Unity for Architectural Visualization

Transform your architectural design into an
interactive real-time experience using Unity

Stefan Boeykens

BIRMINGHAM - MUMBAI

Unity for Architectural Visualization

First published: September 2013

Production Reference: 1190913

Published by Packt Publishing Ltd.
Livery Place
35 Livery Street
Birmingham B3 2PB, UK.

ISBN 978-1-78355-906-0

www.packtpub.com

Cover Image by Mrunal Gawade (mrunal.gawade@gmail.com)

Credits

Author
Stefan Boeykens

Reviewers
Dr. Pieter Jorissen
Dr. Sebastian T. Koenig

Acquisition Editors
Anthony Albuquerque
Kunal Parikh

Lead Technical Editor
Meeta Rajani

Technical Editors
Chandni Maishery
Krishnaveni Nair
Aman Preet Singh

Project Coordinator
Akash Poojary

Proofreaders
Lawrence A. Herman
Lindsey Thomas

Indexer
Mariammal Chettiyar

Production Coordinator
Prachali Bhiwandkar

Cover Work
Prachali Bhiwandkar

About the Author

Stefan Boeykens is an architect-engineer from Leuven, Belgium. After graduation, he was involved in architectural practice for about 4 years, before returning in 2007 to KU Leuven for his PhD on the integration of Building Information Modeling (BIM) in the design process. He worked on a variety of research and education projects, ranging from CAD and BIM, to metadata for architectural archives and cost simulations. His main research interests are BIM 3D modeling, and visualization, digital historical reconstruction, parametric design, programming, and interoperability between a variety of software tools, with a special focus on open BIM.

He is quite literate with software in general, with extensive expertise on ArchiCAD, AutoCAD, SketchUp, Rhinoceros, Excel, Solibri, Processing, CINEMA 4D, Ableton Live, Photoshop, Illustrator, CorelDRAW, Artlantis, and Unity. He likes cross-platform approaches, even more since switching to OS X. Hard disks are always too small for him.

Stefan Boeykens is currently employed by the Department of Architecture at the Faculty of Engineering Sciences at KU Leuven, Belgium. As a teacher, he is responsible for the Architectural Computing courses and teaches students how to use AutoCAD, SketchUp, ArchiCAD, Solibri, CINEMA 4D, Rhinoceros, Grasshopper, and Unity.

He is the author of the `CAD-3D.blogspot.com` blog, which discusses CAD, 3D, and BIM, with a particular interest in free and educational software for architects and interoperability.

Under the name of stefkeB he is active online in various platforms and networks.

He is also a schooled guitar player, both classical and electric, with a keen interest in musical composition in a variety of styles, including progressive rock, pop, metal, electronic experiments, and purely acoustic songs, in English and Dutch, but often also instrumental. As stefkeB, he records everything at home, using Ableton Live mainly. Some of his music can be heard on Soundcloud and Bandcamp. All his compositions are available under a Creative Commons license (CC-BY-NC-SA), by choice.

Unity for architectural visualization is his first actual book, but he has written countless software tutorials; recorded an extensive set of video-tutorials, freely available on Youtube; and has written several academic publications that have been presented on conferences worldwide.

Acknowledgement

This book was a culmination of three years of teaching Unity, learning alongside my students, who weren't always keen on learning "gaming technology" as future professional architects. I thank them for their openness and critical standing, as long as everybody stays positive and constructive. There is more to life than 2D drafting, after all.

I learned a lot from online forums and some of the other Packt Publishing books on Unity, with a special mention to Will Goldstone. I was also inspired by the work of Jon Brouchoud on archvirtual.com, and got some valuable advice from Ivan De Boi and Pieter Jorissen from Karel de Grote University College in Antwerp, and from discussions with former students of mine Thomas Van Bouwel and Berno Bosch on the use of Unity. Several master students are currently applying Unity in some form or other for their master theses, which means I can teach and learn at the same time. The attention to one of my papers on digital reconstruction and the use of game engines was also a clear sign of a growing interest in this subject.

I thank Packt Publishing, especially Akash Poojary and Meeta Rajani, for this opportunity and hope that you, the reader, will really gain something from this book. Sincere thanks to Pieter Jorissen and Sebastian Koenig for their constructive and detailed review. I even learned a thing or two that wasn't clear to me before. Please send me examples of what you were able to accomplish from this.

Finally, I have to express my gratitude to my wife and my three sons, for their support, their love, and their patience. Life in our house is often hectic and time is precious but limited. It is so inspiring to see the unlimited creativity and openness of young children and how they adapt to technology and new concepts. There is no limit to what they would like to create, be it with Lego bricks or in drawings and improvised constructions using whatever they can find in and around the house.

Thank you, all.

About the Reviewers

Dr. Pieter Jorissen finished his computer sciences studies at the Limburg University Center, now known as Hasselt University Belgium, in July 2001. Thereafter, he started working as a researcher at the Expertise Center for Digital Media (EDM) which is the multimedia research center of the UHasselt and is a partner in the IBBT, a Flemish research initiative.

He worked at the EDM for approximately 6 years on several research projects concerning Collaborative Virtual Environments. In January 2008, he obtained his Ph.D. with his dissertation "Dynamic Interactions for Networked Virtual Environments."

In 2008 he mainly worked as a Researcher/Consultant on new technologies and information security for Smals, a large Belgian IT company mostly focusing on supporting the social security administration and eGovernment. His main task was to follow up on new technologies and find ways to implement them for the government administration.

In 2009 he left research and development to start a career as a lecturer at the Karel de Grote University College. He focuses on teaching how to program and build 3D interactive applications. He has also been active as an international program committee member for several computer graphics and virtual reality conferences.

Dr. Sebastian T. Koenig received his Ph.D. in Human Interface Technology from the University of Canterbury, New Zealand, developing a framework for individualized virtual reality cognitive rehabilitation. He obtained his degree as Diploma-Psychologist from the University of Regensburg, Germany, in the areas of Clinical Neuropsychology and Virtual Reality Rehabilitation.

Dr. Koenig is currently working as a Research Associate at the USC Institute for Creative Technologies, where he designs, develops, and tests clinical virtual reality software.

He also works as Lead User Researcher for the game development company Red 5 Studios and as a freelance software engineer and cognitive psychologist to develop mobile applications and cognitive assessments for the US military and health care companies.

His professional experience spans over ten years of clinical work in cognitive rehabilitation and over five years of virtual reality research, development, and user testing. Dr. Koenig has extensive experience as a speaker at international conferences and as reviewer of scientific publications in the areas of Rehabilitation, Cognitive Psychology, Neuropsychology, Software Engineering, Game Development, Games User Research, and Virtual Reality.

Dr. Koenig has developed numerous software applications for cognitive assessment and training. For his work on the Virtual Memory Task he was awarded the Laval Virtual Award 2011, in the category "Medicine and Health." Other applications include the virtual reality executive function assessment in collaboration with the Kessler Foundation Research Center and the patent-pending Microsoft Kinect-based motor and cognitive training JewelMine/Mystic Isle at the USC Institute for Creative Technologies.

Dr. Koenig maintains the website www.virtualgamelab.com about his research and his software development projects. His website also contains a comprehensive list of tutorials for the game engine Unity.

www.PacktPub.com

Support files, eBooks, discount offers and more

You might want to visit www.PacktPub.com for support files and downloads related to your book.

Did you know that Packt offers eBook versions of every book published, with PDF and ePub files available? You can upgrade to the eBook version at www.PacktPub.com and as a print book customer, you are entitled to a discount on the eBook copy. Get in touch with us at service@packtpub.com for more details.

At www.PacktPub.com, you can also read a collection of free technical articles, sign up for a range of free newsletters and receive exclusive discounts and offers on Packt books and eBooks.

http://PacktLib.PacktPub.com

Do you need instant solutions to your IT questions? PacktLib is Packt's online digital book library. Here, you can access, read and search across Packt's entire library of books.

Why Subscribe?

- Fully searchable across every book published by Packt
- Copy and paste, print and bookmark content
- On demand and accessible via web browser

Free Access for Packt account holders

If you have an account with Packt at www.PacktPub.com, you can use this to access PacktLib today and view nine entirely free books. Simply use your login credentials for immediate access.

Table of Contents

Preface   **1**

Chapter 1: An Integrated Unity Workflow   **7**

  Assets and the Unity workflow   **8**

  CAD or 3D modeling software   **8**

    Passing through intermediate software   10

    Expected pitfalls   10

      Missing back-faces   11

      Missing texture coordinates   12

      Superfluous geometry   13

      Lack of instances   14

  Building Information Modeling (BIM) Software   **14**

    Example workflow scenario   15

    Considerations when using BIM software   17

    What about dedicated real-time solutions for CAD/BIM?   18

  Updating the scene when changes occur   **19**

    Optimally supported workflows   21

  Summary   **24**

Chapter 2: Quick Walk Around Your Design   **25**

  Setting up an (almost) empty Unity project   **26**

  Loading up a CAD model   **29**

    Can you show me, please?   29

    Controlling the import settings   31

  Meshes and materials, or Shaders   **33**

  Adding sun light   **34**

  Adding navigation using a first person controller   **35**

  Minding the gap   **36**

  Summary   **37**

Chapter 3: Let There be Light!   **39**

Basic light sources   **39**
Shadows   **40**
  Real-time shadows   40
    Sun study animation   42
    Faking shadows   44
Lightmapping   **46**
  Other lighting techniques   49
  Browsing the Asset Store   50
    Lightmapping packages in the Asset Store   50
Pre-rendered models   **50**
Summary   **52**

Chapter 4: Promenade Architecturale   **53**

First Person versus Third Person Controller   **53**
  Setting up the First Person Controller   54
  Setting up the Third Person Controller   56
  Choosing between FPC and TPC?   58
  Further tweaking and refining the character controllers   59
Loading a custom third person character   **60**
  Using a custom static model   61
  Loading a new character from the Asset Store   61
    Using Mixamo characters and animations   63
Adding a live minimap   **65**
  Switching between cameras?   66
  Setting up a turntable camera animation   67
Displaying basic text/information on the screen   **67**
Summary   **68**

Chapter 5: Models and Environment   **69**

Loading 3D Warehouse models   **70**
Setting up a basic landscape   **71**
  Customizing trees with Tree Creator   71
Creating a custom Skybox   **73**
Optimizing scenes and models   **75**
  Showing only what is needed   76
  Grouping objects by material   76
  Using Prefabs (instancing)   77
  Using Levels of Detail (LOD)   77
  Culling and Batching   78
  Combining Meshes/Children   78

Combining materials (texture atlas)   80
Avoiding excessive collision geometry   81
Summary   **82**

Chapter 6: Shaders and Textures   **83**
  Adjusting basic textured materials   **83**
    Creating convincing glass   85
  Using advanced textured materials   **88**
  Using procedural materials   **91**
    Allegorithmic substances   91
  Learning further material techniques   **92**
    Adjusting texture mapping   93
    Applying animated textures   94
  Summary   **94**

Chapter 7: Full Control with Scripting   **95**
  Scripting crash course   **95**
  Triggering doors and elevators   **96**
    Using triggers and colliders   100
    Refining the opening animation   102
    Moving platforms   103
    Solving a problem with parenting   105
    Rework the script using an animation clip   106
  Basic heads-up-display with a custom GUI   **107**
    Toggling lights and other objects   110
  Switching between cameras   **112**
  Switching between materials   **115**
  Further interactions   **116**
    Resetting the player   116
    Loading another level   118
  Some additional Asset Store tips   **119**
  Summary   **120**

Index   **121**

Preface

This book introduces architects and designers to using Unity for Architectural Visualization. Unity is gaining popularity as a versatile and accessible game authoring system. You get a condensed overview of the workflow between typical architectural design applications and how 3D models exported from those systems can be integrated in real-time environments.

This book takes mostly a hands-on approach and explains the exact steps that are required to complete several aspects of the setup of an interactive, real-time scene. Even though a single introductory book cannot cover everything, you get a complete overview, from the import of 3D models, over improving materials and lighting, up to the writing of several example scripts to add custom interactivity.

While many architects currently rely primarily on traditional 2D drawings and, to a lesser extent, renderings or animations, there is a growing interest in real-time presentations. Led by the development of increasingly complex computer games, many users are familiar with real-time 3D environments. This book cannot possibly teach you how to create a full computer game, but focuses instead on the most important features of computer games to develop compelling, interactive scenes for the so-called *serious games*.

Luckily for you, the reader, such technology has become very accessible and available without any financial investment. Unity is at the forefront of a new generation of game engines, which rival traditional commercial turnkey systems, such as the *Unreal Engine* or *CryEngine*. Interestingly, these other systems have also become more accessible in recent years, probably not by coincidence.

With the examples in this book, you can present to your clients or friends an interactive visit to your own designs and increase your presentation potential.

What this book covers

Chapter 1, An Integrated Unity Workflow, introduces the main concepts of Unity and how it integrates with CAD and BIM software. The concept of Assets and model loading is explained and several recommendations are made about model conversion and file formats to use. This is the most theoretical chapter in the book.

Chapter 2, Quick Walk Around Your Design, explains a complete example going from exporting a 3D model up to adding lighting and navigation, so you can run around freely with very little effort. The following chapters revise these techniques in more detail.

Chapter 3, Let There be Light! shines some light on the scene. You learn about the use of different light sources and shadow calculations. To avoid the heavy burden of real-time shadows, you'll use the Lightmapping technique to bake lights and shadows on the model, from within Unity.

Chapter 4, Promenade Architecturale, explains how you can navigate a 3D character from a third-person perspective. In addition, you will use a second camera to display a mini-map and add overlay information on the screen.

Chapter 5, Models and Environment, discusses the use of models imported from the internet, and the setup of a basic landscape with a custom tree and a skybox environment. There is also an important section on model optimization and performance improvements.

Chapter 6, Shaders and Textures, further dresses up the model. You'll learn about the difference between some of the default shaders and how to integrate an example glass shader. To improve the quality of materials, you will load higher-quality texture maps and experiment with procedural textures.

Chapter 7, Full Control with Scripting, introduces the Unity scripting system and its different scripting languages. We can extend projects with custom functionality writing a few basic short scripts. Some programming experience is helpful, but the examples written in C# are fairly simple and reusable.

What you need for this book

To learn about Unity, you can use any recent version of the Unity game authoring software. This book was written using the free version of Unity 4.2, but the majority of the examples work fine in the previous version, 3.5, of the software. It doesn't matter if you are a Mac or PC user, as they are treated equally by Unity.

Some examples illustrate functionality of the Pro version. To be honest, they were illustrated with the free 30-day trial that you can activate from your free license.

During the writing of the book, two very important updates to Unity became available: the inclusion of the basic iOS and Android add-ons for every Unity license and the addition of real-time shadows in the free version (since release 4.2). Who knows what newer updates will offer...

In addition, you'll need a 3D CAD or Building Information Modeling (BIM) system, such as AutoCAD, ArchiCAD, Revit, Rhino, or SketchUp. Trial-versions are available for all these applications, but chances are that if you are reading this book, you'll be familiar with at least one of them. The examples are elaborated using ArchiCAD and CINEMA 4D, but the concepts translate well to other systems, such as 3ds Max or Maya.

Finally, it is always good to know how to use Photoshop, GIMP or similar image editors.

Who this book is for

This book is primarily written for students and professional architects who know how to model buildings in 3D and have a need to turn their designs into interactive models, even if you never used Unity before.

To be fair, this book is not an introduction to professional game level development, as the methods for highly performing optimized models are often in conflict with the approach of architectural modeling and the constant need for including design changes. The way an architect creates a 3D model of a building is completely different from how a game designer would approach it, for example, using mesh topology optimization, texture atlas editing, or UV unwrapping, applied in non-CAD or BIM software.

Experience with visualization software and programming in any language can be helpful, but is not required to follow along. You will learn all the basics with the step-by-step examples.

Conventions

In this book, you will find a number of styles of text that distinguish between different kinds of information. Here are some examples of these styles, and an explanation of their meaning.

Code words in text are shown as follows: "To react on collisions with a trigger, we use the `OnTriggerEnter` method."

A block of code is set as follows:

```
using UnityEngine;
using System.Collections;
public class loadLevel : MonoBehaviour {
  void Example () {
    Application.LoadLevel("Level1");
  }
}
```

When we wish to draw your attention to a particular part of a code block, the relevant lines or items are set in bold:

```
using UnityEngine;
using System.Collections;
public class loadLevel : MonoBehaviour {
  public string level;
    void Example () {
    Application.LoadLevel(level);
  }
}
```

New terms and **important words** are shown in bold. Words that you see on the screen, in menus or dialog boxes for example, appear in the text like this: "clicking the **Next** button moves you to the next screen".

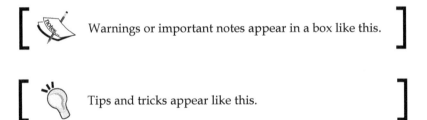

> Warnings or important notes appear in a box like this.

> Tips and tricks appear like this.

Reader feedback

Feedback from our readers is always welcome. Let us know what you think about this book—what you liked or may have disliked. Reader feedback is important for us to develop titles that you really get the most out of.

To send us general feedback, simply send an e-mail to feedback@packtpub.com, and mention the book title via the subject of your message.

If there is a topic that you have expertise in and you are interested in either writing or contributing to a book, see our author guide on www.packtpub.com/authors.

Customer support

Now that you are the proud owner of a Packt Publishing book, we have a number of things to help you to get the most from your purchase.

Downloading the example code

You can download the example code files for all Packt Publishing books you have purchased from your account at http://www.packtpub.com. If you purchased this book elsewhere, you can visit http://www.packtpub.com/support and register to have the files e-mailed directly to you.

Errata

Although we have taken every care to ensure the accuracy of our content, mistakes do happen. If you find a mistake in one of our books—maybe a mistake in the text or the code—we would be grateful if you would report this to us. By doing so, you can save other readers from frustration and help us improve subsequent versions of this book. If you find any errata, please report them by visiting http://www.packtpub.com/submit-errata, selecting your book, clicking on the **errata submission form** link, and entering the details of your errata. Once your errata are verified, your submission will be accepted and the errata will be uploaded on our website, or added to any list of existing errata, under the Errata section of that title. Any existing errata can be viewed by selecting your title from http://www.packtpub.com/support.

Piracy

Piracy of copyright material on the Internet is an ongoing problem across all media. At Packt Publishing, we take the protection of our copyright and licenses very seriously. If you come across any illegal copies of our works, in any form, on the Internet, please provide us with the location address or website name immediately so that we can pursue a remedy.

Please contact us at copyright@packtpub.com with a link to the suspected pirated material.

We appreciate your help in protecting our authors, and our ability to bring you valuable content.

Questions

You can contact us at questions@packtpub.com if you are having a problem with any aspect of the book, and we will do our best to address it.

1
An Integrated Unity Workflow

In this chapter we will explain, how the Unity game authoring system can be integrated into a CAD or BIM-based workflow. It is very important to learn how changes to the design can be propagated into Unity, by fully understanding the asset-based approach inside Unity. The workflow will be illustrated mostly with examples from *Graphisoft ArchiCAD*, *Trimble SketchUp* and *Maxon CINEMA 4D*, but similar workflows can be followed with *Autodesk Revit*, *Maya* and *3ds Max* or even the Open Source *Blender*.

While prior experience with Unity is not required to follow this book, it is recommended that you also follow an introductory Unity tutorial to get started with setting up a project, creating, positioning, and selecting game objects, adjusting properties, and running the game. But don't be afraid, as we will explain the required steps along the road. Some good starting points are given in the first three chapters of the book *Unity 3.x Game Development Essentials* by Will Goldstone (published by *Packt Publishing*) and the *Beginner Editor* official video tutorial series available at `http://unity3d.com/learn/tutorials/modules/beginner/editor`.

This chapter is mostly about workflow, and while filled with important comments, this is for the most part a read only chapter. However, it is important to get a grip on your workflow from modeling to real-time visualization.

In this chapter, we will cover the following topics:

- Assets and the Unity workflow overview
- CAD or 3D modeling software (such as, AutoCAD, SketchUp, Rhino, and Blender)
- BIM software (namely, ArchiCAD and Revit)
- Updating the scene when changes occur to the model

Assets and the Unity workflow

Unity was developed in the context of game development and provides an efficient integration into existing pipelines, independent of the used modeling and content creation software. Regardless if the team consists of you alone or you are part of a large group of designers, developers, artists, and technical directors, you need to get your workflow up and running to be efficient. This is equally relevant for architectural offices, which are also organized around long-running projects where different people interact and collaborate, using a variety of software applications for drafting, modeling, and presentations.

Inside Unity, you create a project, which is stored inside a single folder on your hard disc. Within the project folder, there are a wide variety of folders and files, which are mostly regulated in the background by Unity. The `Assets` folder is where all your files are stored that you need to manage directly, such as models, scripts, textures, and scene files. There is a direct relation between what you see inside the Unity project panel and what occurs as files in your local file system.

Unity also supports additional modules that facilitate the technical aspects of collaboration, for example, by setting the project up with the Asset Server system or by tuning the project metadata (the information about each file) into separate meta-files, that are better suited for **version control systems** (**VCS**), such as Subversion or Git. While such systems are common with software development, they are not widely used in architectural projects. They present an opportunity to share projects between different users, computers, and systems. Using a version control system with Unity, team members can check out files in the project and receive changes from other members. This is more efficient than copying the whole large project folder back and forth since only changes need to be synced. Only the `Assets` and `ProjectSettings` folders need to be synced; other folders are generated locally. More information on using external version control systems with Unity can be found at `http://docs.unity3d.com/Documentation/Manual/ExternalVersionControlSystemSupport.html`, the official Unity documentation website.

CAD or 3D modeling software

Nowadays, it can be assumed that almost any architect or architectural office use CAD or modeling software, such as *Autodesk AutoCAD* or *Nemetschek VectorWorks*, commonly in combination with *Trimble SketchUp*. In addition, we currently see a migration towards **Building Information Modeling** (**BIM**), which will be discussed in the next section.

It should be noted that 2D Drafting is still omnipresent in architectural offices worldwide. While AutoCAD presents both 2D and 3D functionality, many offices still rely on the creation of 2D documents for documentation purposes. The first hurdle they need to tackle in the context of real-time architectural visualization is switching to 3D, as the use of a Game Authoring Environment, such as Unity makes hardly any sense when you don't create 3D models.

As it stands, Unity is mostly oriented to the so-called **Digital Content Creation** (**DCC**) systems, which provide a combination of modeling, rendering, and animation functionality, such as *Autodesk 3ds Max* or *Maxon CINEMA 4D*. Models from such software can be saved directly inside the Unity project's Assets folder and are subsequently converted in the background automatically. When using any of the directly supported software tools, modelers can further edit the models by simply double-clicking the model name from within Unity. This opens the original software, where they can modify the model and save it again, with Unity taking care of the model conversion in the background. This approach is supported by Autodesk 3ds Max and Maya, Maxon CINEMA 4D, Blender, and some other applications given at http://docs.unity3d.com/Documentation/Manual/3D-formats.html. However, most architects will agree that these are not the primary modeling systems in use for architectural modeling.

As it stands, a typical CAD model in for example, AutoCAD DWG format, is not supported by Unity, so you need to convert your model into an alternative format. The FBX format is currently the best supported format for Unity, probably alongside the open COLLADA format, with extension .DAE. If your CAD or 3D software can export one of these two formats directly, use them as your first choice. Otherwise, you can try if your software has 3DS or OBJ export, which are the other two formats that Unity can also read directly. While DXF is supported as well, this is not recommended, as you need to use an older version of the format and texture information will not survive the conversion.

The following table gives an overview of which formats can be exported from some typical CAD software into Unity 4.x and also discusses expected possible problems.

CAD Software	Export	Comments
AutoCAD (DWG)	DWG	Not supported by Unity.
	DXF	Not recommended.
	FBX	Preferred, especially if textures have been applied already.
VectorWorks (VWX)	DXF	Not recommended.
	C4D	*Exchange* add-on recommended; requires CINEMA 4D.
	FBX, DAE	*RenderWorks* add-on required.

CAD Software	Export	Comments
SketchUp (SKP)	FBX	Preferred, but only supported by Pro-version or add-ins.
	DAE	Through Google Earth KMZ export (zipped folder).
	OBJ	Can be added with Ruby script.
Rhino (3DM)	FBX, 3DS, OBJ	Good 3D format support, with control over polygon count and texture mapping.

The primary goal is to get a model on the right scale and with correctly applied materials inside Unity. While not set in stone, the units inside Unity are typically interpreted as being meters. For proper material conversion, support for texturing and the preservation of **UV-texture coordinates** (the way materials are projected onto geometry, which is discussed later on) is essential. While this is common knowledge for visualization artists and game modelers, this is not always the case for CAD users. Most architectural 3D models are created to contain accurate geometry, but present materials as single colors, often tied to the layer on which the object resides.

Passing through intermediate software

If you are in a situation where there is no suitable supported format, you have to rely on 3D conversion software. Even if your CAD system is supported, it makes sense to pass it through other software to fine-tune the conversion. You can export an AutoCAD model as a DWG file into 3ds Max and do the Unity conversion from there.

 While many software combinations are usable, the workflow can be smoother when using a solution from a single software vendor. Going from AutoCAD to 3ds Max or from VectorWorks to CINEMA 4D will ease the conversion, which we will discuss later on.

Expected pitfalls

There are several typical problems that can occur when loading CAD models inside Unity. In most cases, paying attention during modeling can optimize the results considerably.

Missing back-faces

The following screenshot displays a rather typical SketchUp model of the Barcelona Pavillion, by the architect Mies van der Rohe. It was downloaded from the 3D Warehouse and modeled by user *Cintilante 3D* available at `http://sketchup.` `google.com/3dwarehouse/details?mid=fabea878c454e119e8d39fcb58c495` `ea`. When you open the model inside SketchUp, everything looks normal, but when loading it inside Unity, a large part of it seems to be missing at first sight.

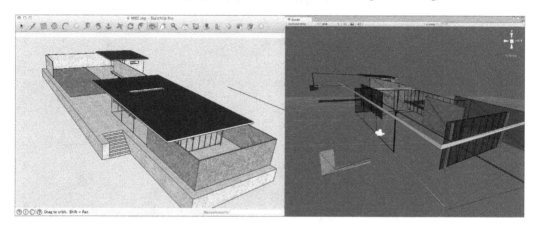

Upon closer inspection, the geometry is actually available in the model, but can only be seen from the other side, for example, from the bottom. CAD software often displays front and back-faces of geometry, whereas Unity hides back-faces for performance reasons (namely, **back-face culling**). The order in which vertices of faces are connected defines the *face orientation*. If you don't pay attention to face orientation during modeling, gaps will appear inside Unity. This problem is not unique to Unity. *Abvent Artlantis*, a rendering companion software often used by architects, also hides back-faces. We have encountered this numerous times when students are trying to import SketchUp models. This is less problematic when you model with volumes or primitive objects, as they are usually well oriented to start with.

The solution is to either display both sides of the geometry, which effectively doubles the geometry to show on screen, or to flip the wrongly oriented faces in the modeling system, which is obviously recommended. In a correct model, only front faces should be visible. In the case of SketchUp, front and back-faces are both visible, but they have different materials applied, which complicates conversion to Unity.

When you model with single faces, this really becomes problematic. The face will only be visible from the front side and is missing completely when looking from the back. If you are modeling fences or other thin elements, such as glass panes, you need to either model them as thin boxes or export the model with faces for both sides separately. If supported, turn off back-face display in the CAD system, to better assess how the model will appear inside Unity. When using SketchUp, switch to the *Monochrome Face Style*, which will show all face orientation mistakes (back-faces) in a light blue color, as shown in the following screenshot:

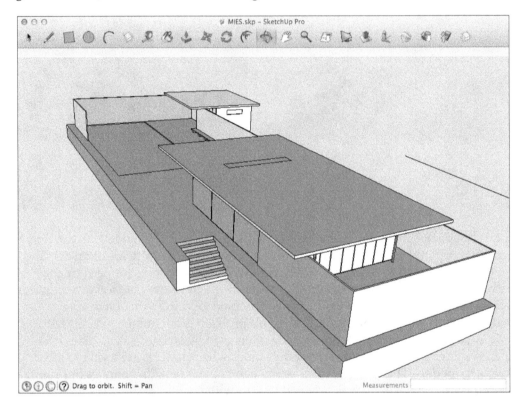

Right click on the problematic faces and choose the **Reverse Faces...** option. Before you export any SketchUp model to Unity, switch to this face style and flip all blue faces. Beware that you might need to re-assign materials, as the front face material will be moved to the other side as well, which is not visible in the Monochrome face style.

Missing texture coordinates

Texture coordinates are the link between a texture image (for example, a picture of a brick wall) and the geometry onto which it is applied. Texture coordinates are stored inside the vertices of geometry, alongside geometric coordinates.

While most game modelers colorize geometry using textures, many architectural models contain plain and solid colors. When exporting to Unity, this becomes a problem, as faces will not have their texture coordinates properly set up. When you assign a material inside Unity or change the **Base (RGB)** texture, it will not be positioned correctly. Chances are that you'll only see a single color, usually the border pixel(s) of the texture or that the position and scale of the texture map on the geometry is inconsistent. The following image displays a basic brick texture and how it is mapped on the imported geometry. The stretched pixels indicate an incorrect mapping setup.

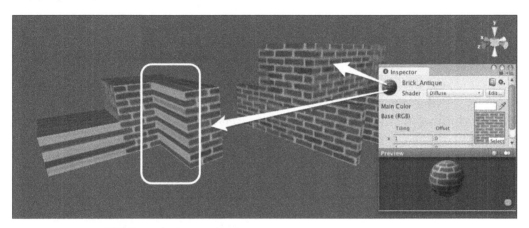

To alter these coordinates from within Unity, Unity requires separate tools and is really cumbersome, certainly when the original model changes. Always assign textures in the original model, even if the texture itself is only a placeholder.

Superfluous geometry

The way models are created for game environments is fundamentally different from the way architectural models are set up. Professional game modelers are trained to use as little geometry as possible. Even though Unity is capable of displaying fairly large and complex models, performance will suffer, so every possible face that is never seen is omitted.

In a CAD model, this is not the case. A door that is placed inside a wall will cover the side of the wall opening, but the faces of this side are still modeled, even if they are never seen. Likewise, cabinets and closets are commonly placed against a wall. If the cabinet never moves, game modelers would remove those faces, whereas architects need them to be visible, as the model can be displayed with or without the covering objects visible.

This problem is harder to solve, as the architectural model has many different purposes. In any case, the architect would need to set up a specific model display to be used when exporting for real-time usage. Such a view needs to hide as much geometry as possible and hide at least those elements that are never to be seen in the real-time model.

It can be valuable to export the CAD or BIM model in chunks, providing more flexibility inside Unity to selectively show or hide parts of the model. Depending on the use case, you could toggle furniture, technical installations, outside walls or even different design alternatives. The next section will show this with the help of an example.

Lack of instances

Most CAD systems support a notion of a *Block* or a *Symbol*. These are objects that occur repeatedly, with identical properties. Typical examples include furniture or sanitary equipment. This technique is called *instancing*, in general. Such objects are used to diminish file sizes and optimize modeling and display performance. Instancing in Unity is organized using *Prefabs*, which are displayed with a blue name in the editor.

However, when converting CAD models to Unity, instancing information often gets lost, depending on the way the export function was implemented. This is something to be tested early on, since it can make a huge difference in performance.

If the export process does not support instancing, it might be beneficial to export only the unique geometry and assemble the model inside Unity, after turning each unique element into a single prefab. For example, in a restaurant project, export a single table into a separate file and load that into your Unity project as a prefab alongside the building geometry. When copying this, all instances will be identical and the system can optimize its performance automatically. This is more efficient than exporting the full scene with all tables included. Beware that this can be a considerable effort, so do this only if required, for example, when the player is able to move or interact with the tables.

Building Information Modeling (BIM) Software

Building Information Modeling or BIM is a methodology of organizing the building process by using digital building models, containing both geometry and information about the entities which comprise a building. The designer creates a three-dimensional model of the building, which embeds information about objects, properties, and relations.

The BIM process is inherently tied to BIM authoring tools, which in the context of this book are typically architectural 3D modeling systems. The best known BIM authoring applications are Graphisoft ArchiCAD and Autodesk Revit and both have been created for this purpose from the beginning. There is also a version of AutoCAD, called *AutoCAD Architecture* that adheres to this concept. There is a wide variety of other software systems for BIM, ranging from modeling (authoring), to viewing, and analysis, but this is beyond the scope of this book.

In the context of architectural visualization, it is important to understand that the modeling process with BIM software is more indirect, when compared to traditional 3D CAD or DCC modeling methods. The user creates building objects, such as walls, floors, and roofs, inserts windows, doors, and other objects, and sets up a variety of views which display the model in some form, such as a 2D annotated drawing, a section or elevation drawing, or a 3D view. The idea is that the model is the main source of all information about the building and all related views are derived from it, just like you would set up a database and create queries that filter information from the model.

The indirect modeling is apparent in the way objects are managed. You start from predefined or custom created parametric objects, which are positioned using only a small set of location parameters: position, orientation, and size mainly. Instead of manipulating 3D geometry directly, you would select the object and change its properties, which triggers a routine that recreates the 3D geometry or other related geometry and characteristics. This also means that there are multiple possible representations of the model. Take this into account when preparing a BIM model for architectural real-time visualization with Unity. You have to decide on many aspects that steer the geometry generation, for example, scale level and building phase or status, alongside a plethora of model display options.

Example workflow scenario

Let's explain this with an example that could be applied in most BIM authoring software applications.

When the architect creates the design, he or she can set up the model in BIM software as an assembly of building entities positioned on stories. At any time, the model can be shown in a 3D view. However, many possible 3D views can be created. Imagine that it has been decided to visualize a first design proposal to the client. The model can be set up at a moderately detailed scale level (for example, 1:100), with the main fixed furniture visible, albeit without some of the model details, such as door knobs and closet handles.

In addition, all technical installations, which have been created as part of the model and which are important mostly for the engineers and contractors, have been hidden in the model. It was decided to mainly show the atmosphere of the design through materials and lights and the layout of the facility.

The particular 3D view is then exported into a Unity compatible format and placed inside a separate folder underneath the project `Assets` folder. We skip the many possible interoperability issues in this example and focus on the overall workflow. Within Unity, the model is imported and positioned in a scene, to be explored in the "game" by the building owner, who receives the Unity project as a standalone application.

Although the architect imagined the building owner not to be interested in the technical details, there are some worries about the feasibility of placing the large ventilation shafts and ducts in a non-obtrusive way, so the architect is asked to update the design. In the BIM authoring system, a new 3D view is created, which only displays the technical installations as 3D geometry and this is exported as a second model for Unity. This model is added to the scene and a small GUI is scripted with two simple buttons to toggle the visibility of the architectural and the installation model upon request. In *Chapter 7, Full Control with Scripting*, we explain how to provide such an option to the user.

After the next client meeting, some design changes are requested. The architect adjusts the model in the BIM authoring software and exports the models again from the two views that have been set up, overwriting the first export files. The model inside Unity is updated automatically and the new version of the interactive application simply has to be built again with identical settings. While the design model changes took some effort, the time it took to update the real-time model inside Unity was negligible.

The scenario pictured here requires some experience to set up a properly, but it is not far-fetched at all and presents an important added value of using BIM authoring software for a real-time architectural visualization. The master model contains the actual, current version of the design, which can be updated at any time, and is completely in sync with the technical drawings, the presentation drawings, or renderings. The real-time model can be updated with minimal effort to integrate changes into Unity. This makes the process accessible in an architectural office, although dedicated visualization teams can create more extensive and graphically refined models, when specializing in the Unity part of the workflow.

Considerations when using BIM software

It is strongly advised to not try to make a single model encompassing every part of the design. It is much more efficient to set up separate complementary models, such as architectural, structural, and technical subsets. They can be assembled inside Unity and toggled from a simple user interface.

While the scenario depicted above seems easy and straightforward, the interoperability poses particular problems. Most BIM software lacks the direct support of the FBX format and even when available, this export is often not optimized for Unity.

Many of the pitfalls we discussed about CAD software are still applicable: architectural BIM models often use plain colors for materials and often lack texture-mapping information.

The problem of back-face culling is less prevalent, as the BIM software tools generate suitable polyhedral meshes where the face orientation is set up properly apart from maybe the glass panes, which are often modeled as a single face only.

There is a huge risk of adding too much geometry into the model, especially when furniture is included or (even worse) if trees and cars are included. While BIM tools often support a good library of common building objects, such as chairs, tables, but also windows and doors, they are typically not set up to minimize geometry. For example, a closet model also contains geometry for the inner parts, even though they are probably never seen in the real-time model, unless the model is set up to allow doors to be opened.

If supported by the BIM software, it is advised to set up the objects to be scale sensitive, allowing them to hide large parts of the geometry when displayed at a larger scale. This can then be used as a setting inside the particular views that have been set up for export to the real-time model. Some applications, such as ArchiCAD also provide a resolution setting for most curved objects, which controls the tessellation into polyhedral meshes.

To make matters worse, the export process often creates each object as a completely new geometric object, disregarding instancing in most cases. If you place 20 chairs in a restaurant space (which is easy to do in a BIM system), each chair will count as separate geometry in the exported model.

If feasible (it often isn't), create separate singular models for such objects and use *Prefabs* inside Unity, which places a much smaller burden on a scene, as repeated geometry will be optimized by the game engine. We will learn more on optimization in *Chapter 5, Models and Environment*.

When trying to add a rotation or sliding animation for doors and windows, it is often impossible to separate the moving parts from the static ones. It may even be necessary to hide them in the model and replace them with custom Unity animated objects, which takes much more effort. As a simple compromise, you can disable collisions on these objects or set them up in their open state in the BIM software, so they don't hinder navigation.

What about dedicated real-time solutions for CAD/BIM?

3D modeling systems and recently BIM authoring software can be extended with plug-ins or add-ons. A good example is the *BIMx* module, developed by Graphisoft, which is integrated into ArchiCAD. It allows a direct export from the ArchiCAD model into a standalone application, including the player and the model. It can be played on a computer (Mac or PC) or loaded into the free BIMx app for Android or iOS devices, allowing real-time navigation through the project, with only minimal effort. The following screenshot displays how an ArchiCAD model looks inside the BIMx software.

Other interesting systems that are worth mentioning are *Autodesk Showcase*, *Act-3D Lumion*, *LightUp* for SketchUp and *Viso3D*, also for SketchUp. There is also *REALIS3D*, which is a dedicated architectural visualization system, built with Unity.

When requiring real-time navigation for a project, it is good to consider such solutions. What they provide in ease-of-use (for example, single click export, built-in features), they often lack customization options. User interaction and the method of navigation are commonly predefined, without the possibility to add other forms of interactivity or visualization.

It is precisely this customization and flexibility that can be the motivation to master a real-time authoring system, such as Unity, at the cost of added effort and complexity. You could re-create most of the functionality of BIMx inside Unity and once this level of interactivity is prepared, using custom scripts, there is nothing preventing you to go a step further. Since this book is about Unity, we will not go into further detail about such dedicated systems.

Updating the scene when changes occur

Regardless if you use CAD or BIM software or rely on DCC systems, chances are that the models need to be updated to reflect changes in the design. Traditional visualization systems often fully import models and convert them in a system specific internal model, which is edited and adapted in a project. However, in such systems, you need to redo all these changes when you have to replace a model with a new, updated version. Since you cannot reasonably assume that a model is completely finalized before any game authoring starts, a more efficient workflow is in order. Like many game authoring systems, Unity is not modeling software, but relies on external software, such as Autodesk 3ds Max or Maxon CINEMA 4D. It is, however, possible to add modeling functionality to Unity using third-party plug-ins, such as *ProBuilder* available at `http://www.probuilder3d.com` or *GameDraw* available at `http://gamedraw.mixeddimensions.com`.

When you load models inside Unity, they are handled by an internal importer module. Like most 3D systems, you can tweak the import with a number of settings. However, in Unity these settings are maintained as part of the imported model's properties and a reference to the original file is kept. Whenever that file is updated, for example by exporting the model again, using the same file name, Unity recognizes this and reloads the file, applying the same import settings again. This is a very important behavior of the Unity pipeline, as you can see that all models that have already been placed inside the different scenes of a project are placed on exactly the same position, at the same scale and using the same geometry conversion. This also allows you to tweak the import, for example, by altering the import settings and re-importing the model even if it has already been placed in scenes of the project.

The following screenshot displays an ArchiCAD model inside Unity:

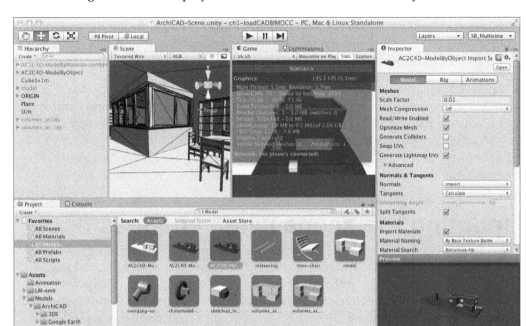

Unity goes a step further when you use one of the directly supported DCC modeling systems, such as 3ds Max, Maya, or CINEMA 4D. If you save your native model directly inside the project's Assets folder, Unity automatically imports the model, or so it seems. Actually, Unity calls the original application in the background to request an export to the FBX format.

If you have such a supported modeling application and it is installed on the same machine as Unity, making changes can be really straightforward as shown:

1. Double click the model icon inside Unity. The native model gets loaded inside the DCC software, ready for you to make changes.

2. When you have finished editing, simply save the file and close the DCC software.

3. When you switch back to Unity, after a few moments, the converted FBX model is reloaded automatically in the background.

For the user, it just looks like there is only a single model that Unity can import when changes occur. This same process also works fine with for example, Photoshop PSD files, where no conversion is required.

When using SketchUp or ArchiCAD or other 3D modeling software that is not directly recognized by Unity, the process is a little more complicated:

1. Double click the model icon inside Unity to launch the authoring software.

2. When you are ready with editing, you need to export the model manually. Export the file to FBX or another supported format and overwrite the previous version in the Unity project's Assets folder.

3. When you switch back to Unity, the model is replaced with the new version.

If you need to set up the conversion configuration each time (for example, when the software does not remember export settings), take care of noting which configuration was used last time. For example, how the model is organized, how textures are treated, and if a possible transformation occurs. Once you have a conversion configuration that works, take a note of all the export settings and be wary of applying them again at the next export action.

Optimally supported workflows

While we would prefer to claim that any modeling software is equally usable, two combinations are worth mentioning specifically and they are based on using software from the same vendor in both cases.

When using CAD or BIM software from Autodesk, it helps to pass through DCC software that is also provided by Autodesk. AutoCAD or Revit models are best passed through 3ds Max or Maya before converting to FBX into Unity. This is especially important to reflect model changes. AutoCAD models are usually passed as DWG files to Max or Maya. Set up correct material properties and texture mapping and either save the file directly inside the Assets folder (to have Unity call up the translation in the background) or export to FBX into the Assets folder. The former is slightly more convenient, but the latter gives you full control and is usually the preferred choice for experienced users.

This is equally true when using software from Nemetschek (or one of its daughter companies). ArchiCAD and VectorWorks models are best passed through CINEMA 4D, before converting to Unity, for exactly the same reason. The *Exchange* plug-ins for ArchiCAD and VectorWorks optimizes the model exchange with CINEMA 4D and automates model updates. You can set up materials and textures and still refine the model in the original creation software. CINEMA 4D models can be placed directly inside the Assets folder.

As always with interoperability through add-ons, success depends on particular software versions and supported platforms and the fact that a software update of one application can break compatibility with the other one. Alas, this is beyond our control.

You can also be confronted with permission problems. When you use the automatic conversion process, Unity copies an FBX exporter module in the supported application's add-on folder, which requires administrative permissions. On Windows, you have to launch Unity as an administrator at least once to have this process completed.

With both the Autodesk and Nemetschek applications workflow, you can reload the architectural model, while preserving applied materials, mapping, or animations, and consequently reload the FBX model inside Unity while preserving the additional settings over there. The following screenshot gives an example of an ArchiCAD model that is exported to CINEMA 4D and loaded inside Unity:

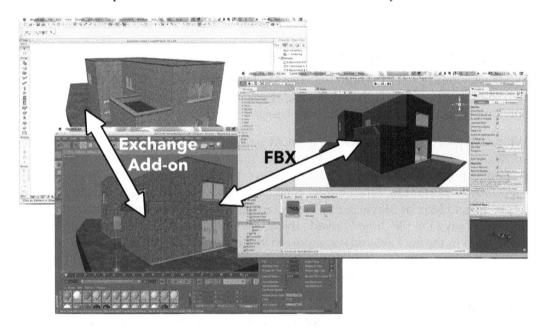

Based on reactions in user forums on Unity (for example, the *Unity Community* at `http://forum.unity3d.com/forum.php`) or one of the related DCC software programs, many people actually suggest ignoring the automatic conversion and leaving the native models (for example, `MAX` or `C4D` files) outside of the `Assets` folder. They would rather perform the conversion manually. This allows more control, for example by splitting the model up in smaller chunks, so they are easier to manipulate inside Unity. This is also required when you collaborate with others and not everyone has the Unity or modeling software available on their machine. In that case, the artist responsible for the 3D model can work on a provided `FBX`, while the designer responsible for the building model can continue working, and export the model when updates need to be integrated.

The following figure summarizes several workflows that are known to work well for architectural visualization. Bold arrows are the recommended pathways for optimal integration.

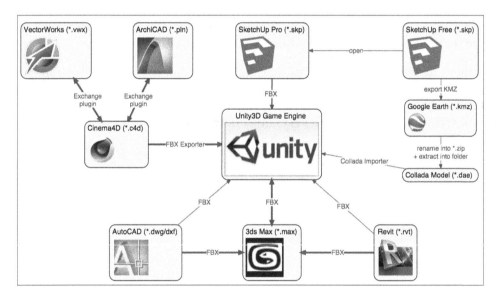

Summary

In this chapter we have talked about the Unity Asset-based workflow. Getting this workflow organized properly is required for working efficiently.

Many architectural projects start from a 2D CAD drawing, in which case there is little you can do inside Unity. If you have a 3D model, made in 3D CAD or BIM software, it is still advised to use a DCC application to pass the model through, to allow fine-tuning of the conversion. At best, this supports a workflow where changes to the design model can still be incorporated in the real-time model, without losing applied interaction inside Unity.

We explained common problems and pitfalls, and collected several tips: apply supported software workflows and formats, use meters as units, set up normals correctly, always apply textures, export models in chunks, and avoid excessive geometry.

Further chapters will explain the actual process in more detail, from simply getting started, to full control over graphic quality and interaction.

So without further delay, fire up your modeling software of choice and ensure you have a copy of Unity installed and activated, either the free or the pro-version. In the next chapter, we will load our project in Unity and add the necessary interactivity to walk around in real-time with very little effort, using functions that are installed with Unity.

2
Quick Walk Around Your Design

This chapter will briefly go over the full process of loading a CAD or BIM model in Unity, setting up scaling and colliders, adapt some common materials, and add a general lighting setup. We add a basic navigational control setup to walk around, and hit play to walk around our design.

Further chapters will go into more detail on how to improve the visual quality and how to add more interactivity, but if you have time for only one single chapter, this chapter will at least get your project in a usable state, with only a minor effort.

In this chapter, we will cover:

- Project setup
- Loading a model
- Meshes and materials, or shaders
- Adding sun light
- Add navigation

Setting up an (almost) empty Unity project

The first thing you need to ensure is that you have a 3D model that you want to explore and you have a way to export it into one of the Unity supported formats. Please revisit *Chapter 1, An Integrated Unity Workflow*, to get more insight into this workflow.

When you launch Unity, by default it loads the last project you worked on. If this is a fresh install, this is usually the sample project called *AngryBots* that was installed, but while impressive, it is way too elaborate to use as a starting point. Start this chapter by creating a new, empty project by navigation to **File | New Project...**, which opens the **Project Wizard** as shown in the following screenshot. To open this wizard directly, hold the *Alt* key while launching Unity.

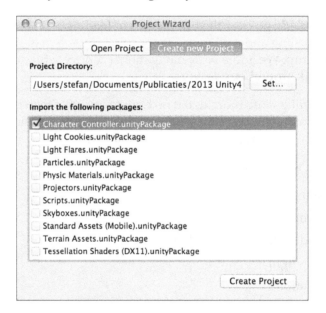

From this dialog, we can import *Packages* that have been installed with Unity. Packages are compressed files that contain a series of ready-to-use *Assets*. Check the **Character Controller** package for this example and skip the others. Name the project anything you want. When you press **Create Project**, you will see a loading screen, which prepares the project for you, including the installation of chosen packages. Next, you will see an empty Unity project, with the default GUI layout loaded, as shown in the following screenshot:

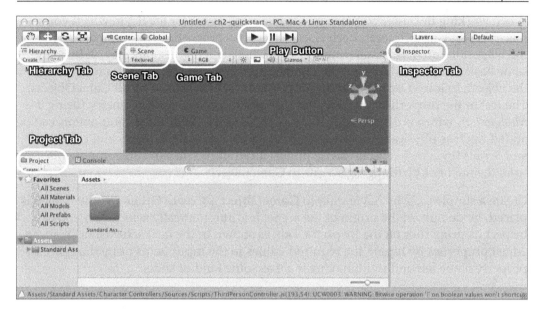

The GUI contains different tabbed windows and can be completely reorganized, to optimize screen space depending on your activity (for example, modeling, animation, lighting and so on). The main tabs present the information inside your project. These tabs are explained in the following points:

- **Hierarchy Tab:** This tab displays the content of the current *Scene*, which is usually a level in the game, but it can also be a loading screen or menu.

- **Scene Tab:** This tab is the 3D graphical view on the geometry inside the scene. This will be quite familiar if you come from CAD or 3D modeling software.

One caveat! Like most 3D software, a coordinate system is displayed as three colored axes in Red, Green, and Blue, being X, Y, and Z respectively. But unlike most CAD systems, Unity uses the Y-axis as upward direction instead of Z!

- **Inspector Tab:** This tab displays the properties of any selected object, either from the Scene Tab or from one of the other tabs.

- **Project Tab:** This tab is (almost) a direct view on the `Assets` folder, as it displays all files a users needs to manage in a project. There are some additional hidden files and users are urged to only use the Unity interface to rename assets or move them around.

- **Game Tab:** This tab is a preview of how the scene will look from the camera when you play the game, by pressing the triangular **Play button** on the upper toolbar.

When working in Unity, you manage one or more *scenes* (or levels) in which you place several **GameObjects**. Each GameObject has properties you can manage using the Inspector Tab. The actual properties vary between objects, but they all have the same basic structure, starting with a name and some metadata (information about the object), followed by the `Transform` property, which is used by all GameObjects. The rest of the properties can vary, but they often contain some geometry (using a *Mesh Filter*), which is displayed using a *Mesh Renderer*. Additional components can be added, such as physical properties (so that objects can react to forces and collisions) and *Scripts* (by which objects can do almost anything). You can add components from the menu or by dragging scripts to GameObjects.

Create a simple *Cube* by navigating to **GameObject | Create Other | Cube**, which is placed, by default, in the origin of the scene. It is automatically selected so you can inspect its properties on the Inspector Tab, as shown in the next screenshot. You can adjust properties by typing the required values in the input fields or by dragging the property name left and right, having it act as some kind of slider.

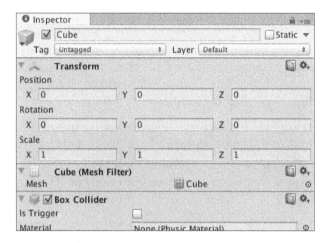

While we said we would be loading one of our own models, it is advisable to also load a basic cube with scale values of 1 for each axis. In Unity, this creates a cube of size 1x1x1 meter.

To be clear, Unity does not really enforce any particular unit size, but it is quite common to relate everything to meters. The cube will help us to assess the scale of an imported CAD or 3D model.

Loading up a CAD model

Whatever the program or workflow you use, you need to save a 3D model in a format Unity recognizes. You either save the model directly inside the Assets folder from within your modeling software **Save As…** or **Export…** dialog, but you can also drag the file onto the Unity project window. The end result is the same.

Can you show me, please?

We will illustrate this using Graphisoft ArchiCAD and Maxon CINEMA 4D. The workflow when using Autodesk Revit or AutoCAD in combination with 3ds Max is similar.

Since you cannot export from ArchiCAD to the recommended FBX or Collada formats directly, you need conversion software. While many modeling systems, including ArchiCAD, support exporting to 3DS (old 3D Studio for DOS format, before 3ds Max was created) or OBJ (old Alias Wavefront format, before Maya was released), these formats present certain limitations and make the update process cumbersome.

In the particular combination of ArchiCAD and CINEMA 4D, it is advised to use the *Exchange add-on*, which enables the C4D format export from ArchiCAD. The clever part is that changes in the ArchiCAD model can be exported again and be merged inside CINEMA 4D, which effectively replaces the old geometry with the new version, but retaining assigned or altered materials and all other settings, such as lights, cameras, additional models, animations, or rendering settings. When you export your ArchiCAD Model, you have two options in the **CINEMA 4D Settings** dialog inside ArchiCAD by navigating to **Design | Design Extras | Cinema 4D Exchange | CINEMA 4D Settings,** to go **by Material** or to go **by Class (Wall, Slab, etc.)**. We keep the **Geometry scaling factor** at **1,00**. This is shown in the following screenshot:

The first option makes it easier inside CINEMA 4D to adjust materials, as the model is structured in groups, in which each group has one material **tag** assigned, as shown in the following screenshot, displaying the **Objects** browser. This works fine inside CINEMA 4D, as the material properties are passed to child objects, unless they contain their own material tag.

As we have experienced, this presents a problem once inside Unity. The exact hierarchy of groups and objects is recreated with GameObjects. The groups inside Unity will become empty GameObjects, which do not contain any material. The actual meshes are placed as children underneath the groups, using a default, grey **No Name** material, thus making the model unusable inside Unity.

You can use a utility function inside newer versions of CINEMA 4D to re-organize the model structure to actually combine all meshes, and properly assign the material by navigating to **Tools | Combine Project**. The following screenshot shows the effect of the **By Material** option:

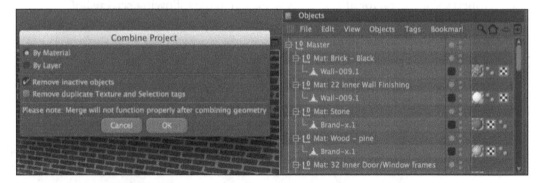

As a result, the model hierarchy is shifted around and is now suitable for export to Unity.

Beware that you can no longer use the *Merge* function in CINEMA 4D when the original model is changed, as this depends on a pre-defined model structure, so if you plan on updating the original model, it is best to retain the original structure and stick to the **By Class** option in the CINEMA 4D export dialog, as it works better inside Unity.

To go from CINEMA 4D to Unity can be done in two ways. When you export the C4D file directly inside the Assets folder, Unity loads up CINEMA 4D in the background and automatically exports the project to an FBX file. This is the simplest workflow. You can even double-click the model in the Unity Project Tab to open it up in the native software, make changes, save, and close, and the placed model is updated automatically. The second approach, as suggested by most experts, is doing it manually, by keeping the native model outside of the Assets folder and exporting to FBX when needed. This gives more control and flexibility.

Controlling the import settings

When the model is loaded inside Unity, it is displayed inside the Project Tab. If you click on the model name or icon, you can adjust the import settings in the Inspector Tab, as shown in following screenshot:

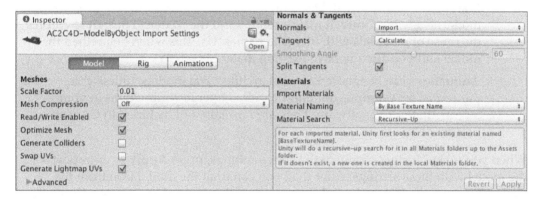

The settings are explained in the following points:

- The first and foremost important setting is the **Scale Factor**. While you can scale any imported and positioned object using the transform component of placed GameObjects, this sometimes has unexpected effects on, for example, child object transformations. You should try to adjust the scaling factor on the model importer to ensure that it can be instanced in the scene using a transform scale of X=1, Y=1, and Z=1. This is directly dependent on how the model was exported. We usually apply a scale of 1, 0.1 or 0.01, which is easy to find out using trial and error.

- **Mesh Compression** is mostly meant for large organic meshes. We try to avoid any change that would alter the mesh structure, so we leave this unchecked. **Optimize Mesh** does not change the look of the mesh, so it can be safely checked.

- If you need your character to be able to walk on top of geometry and climb staircases, you should enable **Generate Colliders**. This uses the actual geometry to create a *Mesh Collider* for each object.

> While not the most efficient approach, performance-wise, the only real alternative is to use a separate simplified model as a collision mesh. Replace the Mesh collider in complex objects, such as plants or furniture, with a simple box or cylinder, to increase collision efficiency. This is done in professional game authoring, to increase efficiency and performance, but is often unfeasible in our context of architectural building models.

- **Generate Lightmap UVs** is required if you want to use Unity's integrated *Beast Lightmapping*. We could ignore it for our quick test, as it makes the import process longer, but we'll make use of it in the next chapter.

- **Normals & Tangents** are left at their default settings.

- **Materials** will be created, based on the model structure. If you have multiple models loaded in Unity, it makes sense to set the **Material Search** to enforce the reuse of materials with identical names. Use this when you reload the model and you already have existing materials set up.

- **Animations** can be ignored in most architectural models, unless you did record for example, door and window opening animations in your intermediate DCC software. They are normally not included in CAD or BIM models.

When you make changes to any of the above settings, press **Apply** to re-import the model with these settings. After that, you can drag the model icon from the Project Tab onto the Hierarchy Tab or directly in the Scene view. We usually set the transform of the model to be in the origin (*X=0, Y=0, and Z=0*) and work from there.

The first thing you need to do is compare your model scale with a reference object. Use the *Cube* object we placed earlier and move it close to the model, so you can check if your scale looks fine.

Resist the urge to press **Play** at this moment, since without any further action, you cannot interact with the scene right now. You can however inspect the model directly in the Scene view, by panning and orbiting around.

Use the Hand icon (see previous screenshot) by clicking on it with the *Left Mouse Button* (*LMB*) to pan around and press *Alt* + *LMB* to switch to orbit mode. The *mouse wheel* zooms in and out. While similar to typical 3D or CAD software, beware that the modifier keys are probably not exactly the same as what you are used to. After a while, it becomes second nature, luckily. As an alternative, the *Q*, *W*, *E*, and *R* keys are mapped to these four tools respectively.

Meshes and materials, or Shaders

Select the model in the Hierarchy Tab and fold out the small triangle to see the hierarchical outline of parent and child objects. When you select any of the child objects, it usually has a **Mesh Filter** containing the geometry, a **Mesh Renderer**, which has shadow settings and a list of assigned materials. For each material there is a separate **Materials** component, which displays the material properties. This is shown in the following screenshot:

 Beware that materials are shared between objects, so adjustments are effective on all objects that reference this material.

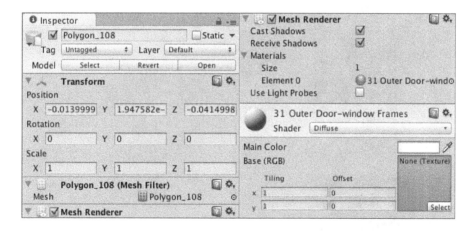

Most materials use the basic **Diffuse** shader or material definition and we will leave them for now. You could tweak the material for glass objects a bit, to emulate something more reflective, but we will look at this in more detail in *Chapter 6, Shaders and Textures*.

You can adjust the *tiling* and *offset* of the material component, but this has effect on every geometric object where this material is used. Keep this in mind if you try to load other materials!

If you try to play the scene right now, nothing will happen, yet.

Adding sun light

Without lighting the scene looks quite dark and dull. For architectural scenes and environments, you probably need a sun-like light source. We will add a *Directional Light* by navigating to **GameObject | Create Other | Directional Light**. This is a light source that emits light in one particular, parallel direction. Its position does not matter.

Press *E* to activate the **Rotation** tool and drag the colored circles of the *Rotate Gizmo* to point it downward, as direction is very important. This can be seen in the following screenshot:

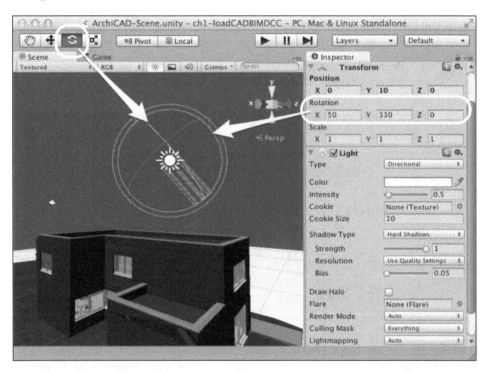

While we said that position doesn't matter, it often makes sense to place the Directional Light slightly above the scene, with the rays pointing towards your design, as a visual clue for yourself.

You can adjust **Color** and **Intensity** to your liking. Slightly yellow with intensity between 0.5 and 1 is a good starting point. You can also activate the **Shadow Type**, which enables real-time shadows. Beware that this can be computationally expensive. Further setup will be the topic of *Chapter 3, Let There be Light!*

We are almost ready to press play. We promise!

Adding navigation using a first person controller

In most interactive 3D environments, you have a basic choice of two main navigational configurations when you want to walk around: *first* and *third person perspective*.

When Unity is installed, it comes with a set of packages that add assets for common tasks. If you forgot to check the **Character Controller** package when we initiated the game project, you can still do so from the Assets menu by navigating to **Assets | Import Package | Character Controller**.

In the Project tab, you can find the **First Person Controller (FPC)** in the **Standard Assets | Character Controller** folder. Drag it onto the **Hierarchy** or **Scene** window. Position it using the Move and Rotate gizmos where you want to start in the scene and ensure the bottom side of the **Capsule** geometry is slightly above the ground, to avoid falling through into the oblivion.

If there is no ground geometry in your project, you could add a **Plane** GameObject with Transform Position **Y**=0, to act as a simple ground plane. As shown in the following screenshot:

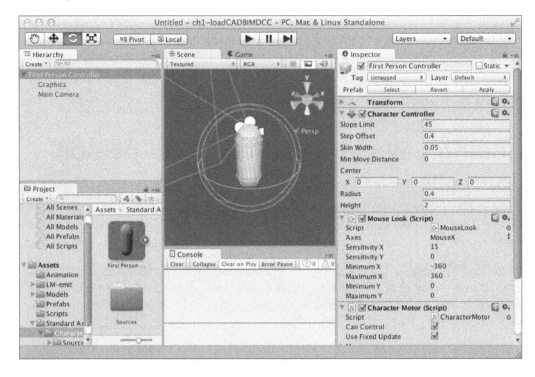

The FPC is loaded as a *Prefab*, which makes it reusable in other scenes, indicated by a blue name in the Hierarchy Tab.

Now you can finally play the scene! This can be done by pressing play or by pressing *Ctrl + P* on Windows, or on Mac OS X by pressing *Command + P*. Walk around using the arrow keys and choose the viewing direction using the mouse. Press the *Space* key to jump up.

Minding the gap

While the above sections are a minimal but complete overview of how to set up an interactive walk around your architectural model, some additional recommendations and tips are valuable, such as:

- To walk around your model, provide a terrain or at least a slab to walk on. As an alternative, you can use a *Plane* or *Quad* GameObject or, even better, a **Unity Terrain**.

- When you notice your character cannot get up the stairs or onto a slope, you will have to adjust the properties of the **Character Controller** component of the FPC, such as **Step Offset** and **Slope Limit**.

- When you can see through the walls when you get too close to it, lower the **Near Clipping Plane** of the *Camera* component.

- If your character cannot pass through a door opening, try lowering the **Radius** of the **Character Controller** component.

- Unity sometimes freezes when characters collide with geometry that is too complex, for example, plants or furniture objects with a full *Mesh collider*. Replace the collider with a simplified one, such as a *Box* or *Cylinder Collider*.

We will refine this setup and compare it with a *Third Person Controller* in *Chapter 4, Promenade Architecturale*. Refer to that chapter, if you encounter problems or need more detail.

Summary

There we are. We made a complete, free-roaming, real-time environment from a CAD or BIM model. That was not too hard, was it?

When all you need is a quick walk through around a CAD model, this chapter will help you a lot. This chapter explained the basic steps of exporting your model into Unity and adding a sun and a navigation control system.

It is wise to have a fast and predictable recipe, as it usually works out fine, especially when you are pressed by a deadline looming around the corner. This basic setup is the minimum that is required for an interactive scene.

Job done? Not quite. What we have shown in this quick overview might be impressive for your very first project, but if it is needed to sell a design, there is much more to it! The next chapter will start with getting a better lighting setup, including shadows.

3
Let There be Light!

Adding a basic directional light is a simple start, as illustrated in *Chapter 2, Quick Walk Around Your Design*. However, chances are that you expected much more from a game engine like Unity. The basic lights only get you so far. While the free version of Unity lacks some of the features of the pro-version, we will show you how you can still get convincing lighting in your project. After all, if all you would get looks flat and dull, why use Unity in the first place?

In this chapter, we will cover:

- Basic lights
- Shadows
- Lightmapping
- Using pre-rendered models (Lightbaking in an external software)

Basic light sources

You use lights to give a scene brightness, ambience, and depth. Without light, everything looks flat and dull. Use additional light sources to even-out lighting and to set up interior scenes. In Unity, lights are components of GameObjects. The different kinds of light sources are as follows:

- **Directional lights**: These lights are commonly used to mimic the sun. Their position is irrelevant, as only orientation matters. Every architectural scene should at least have one main Directional light. When you only need to lighten up an interior room, they are more tricky to use, as they tend to brighten up the whole scene, but they help getting some light through the windows, inside the project. We'll see a few use cases in the next few sections.

- **Point lights**: These lights are easy to use, as they emit light in any direction. Try to minimize their Range, so they don't spill light in other places. In most scenes, you'll need several of them to balance out dark spots and corners and to even-out the overall lighting.

- **Spot lights**: These lights only emit light into a cone and are good to simulate interior light fixtures. They cast a distinct bright circular light spot so use them to highlight something.

- **Area lights**: These are the most advanced lights, as they allow a light source to be given an actual rectangular size. This results in smoother lights and shadows, but their effect is only visible when baking and they require a pro-license. They are good to simulate light panels or the effect of light coming in through a window. In the free version, you can simulate them using multiple Spot or Directional Lights.

Shadows

Most current games support some form of shadows. They can be pre-calculated or rendered in real-time. *Pre-calculation* implies that the effect of shadows and lighting is calculated in advance and rendered onto an additional material layer. It only makes sense for objects that don't move in the scene. *Real-time shadows* are rendered using the GPU, but can be computationally expensive and should only be used for dynamic lighting. You might be familiar with real-time shadows from applications such as SketchUp and recent versions of ArchiCAD or Revit.

Ideally, both techniques are combined. The overall lighting of the scene (for example, buildings, street, interiors, and so on) is pre-calculated and baked in texture maps. Additional real-time shadows are used on the moving characters. Unity can blend both types of shadows to simulate dynamic lighting in large scenes. Some of these techniques, however, are only supported in the pro-version.

Real-time shadows

Imagine we want to create a sun or shadow study of a building. This is best appreciated in real-time and by looking from the outside. We will use the same model as we did in the previous chapter, but load it in a separate scene. We want to have a light object acting as a sun, a spherical object to act as a visual clue where the sun is positioned and link them together to control the rotations in an easy way. The steps to be followed to achieve this are as follows:

1. Add a Directional light, name it `SunLight` and choose the **Shadow Type**. **Hard shadows** are more sharply defined and are the best choice in this example, whereas **Soft shadows** look smoother and are better suited for a subtle, mood lighting.

2. Add an empty GameObject by navigating to **GameObject | Create Empty** that is positioned in the center of the scene and name it `ORIGIN`.

3. Create a Sphere GameObject by navigating to **GameObject | Create Other | Sphere**, name it `VisualSun`.

4. Make it a *child* of the **ORIGIN** by dragging the **VisualSun** name in the **Hierarchy** Tab onto the **ORIGIN** name.

> Children are linked to their parent object and follow the parent's transformation. Parent-Child relations are indicated in the **Hierarchy** Tab using small triangles, which you can collapse or fold out. Children are displayed below and slightly to the right of their parent. The next screenshot highlights an actual example.

5. Give it a bright, yellow material, using a **Self-Illumin/Diffuse Shader**. Deactivate **Cast Shadows** and **Receive Shadows** on the **Mesh Renderer** component.

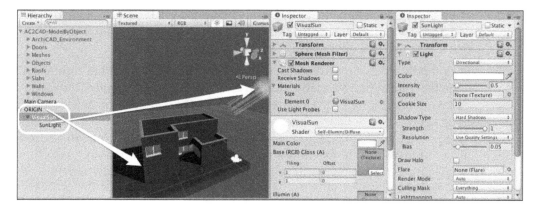

6. After you have placed the **VisualSun** as a child of the origin object, reset the position of the Sphere to be 0 for **X, Y** and **Z**. It now sits in the same place as its parent. Even if you move the parent, its *local* position stays at **X**=0, **Y**=0 and **Z**=0, which makes it convenient for a placement relative to its parent object. Alter the Z-position to define an offset from the origin, for example 20 units. The negative Z will facilitate the SunLight orientation in the next step.

7. The **SunLight** can be dragged onto the **VisualSun** and its local position reset to zero as well. When all rotations are also zero, it emits light down the Z-axis and thus straight to the origin.

8. If you want to have a nice *glow* effect, you can add a *Halo* by navigating to **Components | Effects | Halo** and then to **SunLight** and setting a suitable **Size**.

We now have a hierarchic structure of the origin, the visible sphere and the Directional light, that is accentuated by the halo. We can adjust this assembly by rotating the origin around. Rotating around the Y-axis defines the orientation of the sun, whereas a rotation around the X-axis defines the *azimuth*. With these two rotations, we can position the sun wherever we want.

> Mastering parent-child relations is important for effective scene organization.

Sun study animation

To automate movement in a game, we can use either an animation clip or a custom script. We'll show an animation clip in the following example:

1. Before we start defining the animation, ensure the **ORIGIN** is selected. Also open an **Animation** Tab by navigating to **Window | Animation** and dock it somewhere convenient.

2. There are different ways to create an animation clip. You can either right-click on the timeline in the **Animation** Tab or click on the second popup (the menu displays **[Create New Clip]**) just above the object tree in the same window. A dialog opens asking you to name the new animation clip, so name it **SunPath**. This is an Asset, which is stored as a file in the `Assets` folder. You will also see that an **Animation** component is added to the **ORIGIN** GameObject, which points to the **SunPath** animation clip we just created. This is shown in the following screenshot:

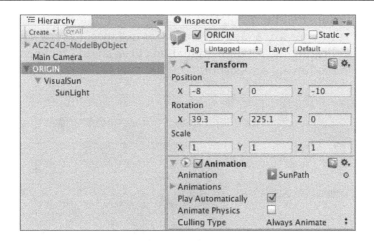

You can also create an Animation Clip from the menu by navigating to **Assets | Create | Animation** but then you need to add the Animation component to the **ORIGIN** object and select the **SunPath** clip or simply drag the clip on the object.

3. Now the clip is ready to record *keyframe animation* in the Animation Tab. This should immediately make sense to anyone familiar with 3D animation software or other tools, such as Adobe Flash. We'll follow the step-by-step procedure given as follows:

    1. Click on the small circle icon on the right side of the **Rotation.y** parameter and select **Add Curves**, which creates new *Animation Curves* for the rotations (we always have the three of them included).

    2. Drag the *timeslider* (the red vertical line) to time 0:00 and add a *key/keyframe* by right-clicking on the dark grey area underneath the timeline and select **Add Keyframe**. As long as the red recording button is active, you can adjust the timeslider and change rotation values in the transform component, so keyframes will be added automatically.

3. Ensure that the Y-rotation is 0 degrees at timestep 0:00 and that it is 360 degrees at a later timestep (for instance, 02:00). The yellow line indicating the rotation animation curve should be linear, as shown in the following screenshot:

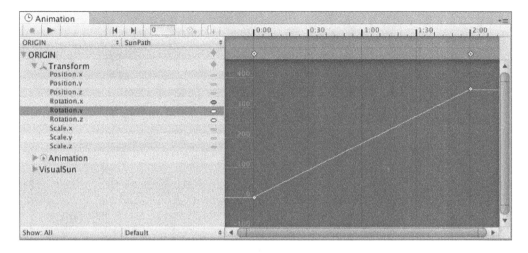

4. Select the SunPath clip in the Project tab to display its properties and set the **wrap mode** of the Animation Clip in the Inspector Tab to "**loop**" so it will repeat in a cycle.

4. The animation clip is now attached to the Origin and it plays if you run the game (**Play Automatically** parameter is set to true in the Animation component) or if you press the triangular play button in the Animation Tab.

For a more elaborate sun study, also animate the X-rotation (or azimuth), the intensity, and the color of the Sun.

Animation clips can be reused with other objects and in other scenes.

To reuse this setup in other scenes, turn the whole hierarchy into a *Prefab*. To export it into other projects, consider exporting it as a *Package*.

Faking shadows

A *Blob Shadow* is a cheap way to add a hint of a shadow. A special bitmap is projected and when positioned correctly appears, for example, underneath the feet of your main character, as we show it in the following steps. This requires fewer resources than using real-time shadows.

1. Load the **Projectors** package by navigating to **Assets | Import Package | Projectors**, which contains a few materials, shaders, and prefabs to get you started.

2. Drag the **Blob Shadow Projector** prefab onto the scene. This contains a Projector component, which acts similar to a light source, but uses a material. The following **Inspector** screenshot shows the material being set up using the **Projector/Multiply** shader and a **Cookie** texture of a black blurred circle on a white background.

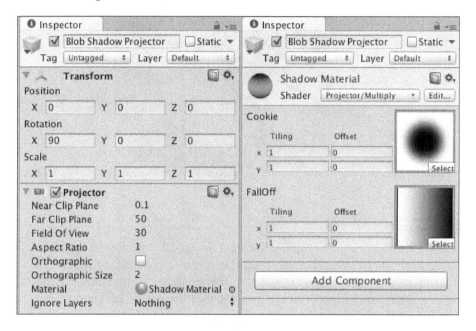

3. Position this Projector above our third person character using the transformation gizmo, so it projects a soft dark-grey circle.

4. To avoid casting a shadow onto the character, increase the **Near Clip Plane** parameter of the Projector so the shadow starts just underneath the feet of our character (for example, 3 units). The **Far Clip Plane** is usually big enough by default.

5. To ensure the Projector follows the character wherever it goes, you can use a short script or simply drag the Projector as a child object of the character, as illustrated in the following screenshot:

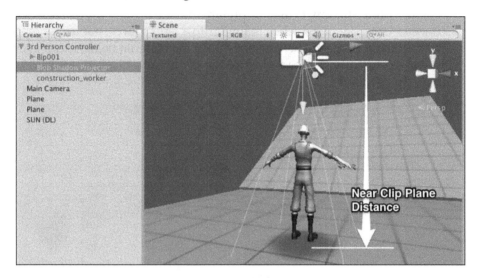

Lightmapping

Real-time lighting is computationally very expensive. If you don't have the latest hardware, it might not even be supported. Or you might avoid it for a mobile app, where hardware resources are limited. It is possible to pre-calculate the lighting of a scene and *bake* it onto the geometry as textures. This process is called **Lightmapping**, for more information on it visit:

http://docs.unity3d.com/Documentation/Manual/Lightmapping.html

While actual calculations are rather complex, the process in Unity is made easy, thanks to the integrated *Beast Lightmapping*. There are a few things you need to set up properly. These are given as follows:

1. First, ensure that any object that needs to be baked is set to *Static*. Each GameObject has a static-toggle, right next to the Name property. Activate this for all models and light objects that will not move in the Scene.

2. Secondly, ensure that all geometry has a second set of texture coordinates, called UV2 coordinates in Unity. Default GameObjects have those set up, but for imported models, they usually need to be added. Luckily for us, this is automated when **Generate Lightmap UVs** is activated on the model import settings given earlier in *Chapter 2, Quick Walk Around Your Design*, in the section entitled, *Controlling the import settings*.

3. If all lights and meshes are static and UV2 coordinates are calculated, you are ready to go. Open the **Lightmapping** dialog by navigating to **Window | Lightmapping** and dock it somewhere conveniently.

There are several settings, but we start with a basic setup that consists of the following steps:

1. Usually a **Single Lightmap** suffices. **Dual Lightmaps** can look better, but require the *deferred rendering* method that is only supported in Unity Pro.

2. Choose the **Quality High** modus. **Quality Low** gives jagged edges and is only used for quick testing.

3. Activate **Ambient Occlusion** as a quick additional rendering step that darkens corners and occluded areas, such as where objects touch. This adds a real sense of depth and is highly recommended. Set both sliders somewhere in the middle and leave the distance at 0.1, to control how far the system will look to detect occlusions.

4. Start with a fairly low **Resolution**, such as 5 or 10 **texels per world unit**. This defines how detailed the calculated Lightmap texture is, when compared to the geometry. Look at the **Scene** view, to get a checkered overlay visible, when adjusting Lightmapping settings. For final results, increase this to 40 or 50, to give more detail to the shadows, at the cost of longer rendering times.

There are additional settings for which Unity Pro is required, such as **Sky Light** and **Bounced Lighting**. They both add to the realism of the lighting, so they are actually highly recommended for architectural visualization, if you have the pro-version.

On the **Object** sub-tab, you can also tweak the shadow calculation settings for individual lights. By increasing the radius, you get a smoother shadow edge, at the cost of longer rendering times. If you increase the *radius*, you should also increase the amount of *samples*, which helps reduce the noise that gets added with sampling. This is shown in the following screenshot:

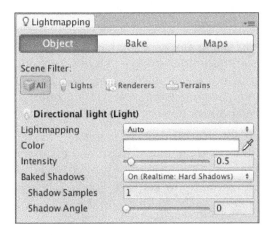

Now you can go on and click **Bake** Scene. It can take quite some time for large models and fine resolutions. Check the blue time indicator on the right side of the status bar (but you can continue working in Unity). After the calculations are finished, the model is reloaded with the new texture and baked shadows are visible in Scene and Game views, as shown in the following screenshot:

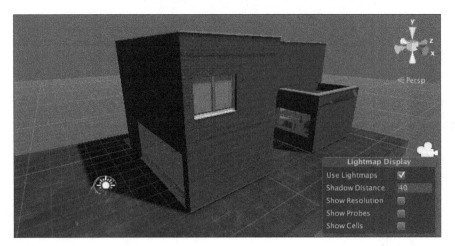

Beware that to bake a Scene, it needs to be saved and given a name, as Unity places the calculated Lightmap textures in a subfolder with the same name as the Scene.

Other lighting techniques

You can get pretty far using the default lights and the Lightmapping technique. But there is more to get convincing or downright spectacular lighting in Unity. While many of these techniques rely on a Unity Pro license, sometimes you can fake these if you understand what the effect is trying to achieve.

- It is possible to have a material emit light, if you use a self-illuminated shader (**Self-Illumin/Diffuse**). While the material in itself seems to glow and you could add a *Halo* component to increase the effect, only Unity Pro will take their actual light into account when Lightmapping. To partially fake this effect in Unity Free, combine a self-illuminated material with one or more spotlights positioned in the same place and which emit a matching color.

- While Unity Pro has a **Skylight** option in the **Lightmapping** dialog, you can fake environmental lighting by adding some additional, bluish Directional lights in opposite directions around the model. Turn down their brightness and add soft shadows with a 15-degree shadow radius and about 12 samples. These lights brighten up dark shadows with a blueish-cool tint, mimicking the effect of the ambient light that gets scattered from the sky. Try to avoid dark-black shadows, unless you model a Moon scene.

- Using a *Light projector*, like we did for the Blob Shadow, we can also project any image onto the scene. This can simulate the effect of light shining through tinted glass windows or piercing through a silk screen.

If you have a pro-license, there is also a series of *Fullscreen Image Effects* that you can add to the Camera. They help to give your scenes a more polished effect and since they run mostly on the GPU, they don't slow down the scene too much. The following effects are recommended:

- **Anti-aliasing**: It increases the apparent resolution by smoothing edges.

- **Bloom** and **Lens Flares**: Bloom adds a white, dreamlike glow, whereas the lens flares present a dramatic accent to the main light source. These effects are automatically generated in a highly efficient way (if you promise not to overdo it!).

- **Color Correction** and **Tonemapping**: It is used for color balancing, which is useful to avoid a cheap, artificial color palette.

- **Screen Space Ambient Occlusion (SSAO)**: It is used to mimic the effect of small occlusions an inter-object shadows, which increases the realism of the scene and accentuates the volumetric properties of objects.

More info is available at: `http://docs.unity3d.com/Documentation/Components/`
`comp-ImageEffects.html`

Browsing the Asset Store

While Unity includes a few packages with additional assets (scripts, models, textures and so on), there is a fully integrated store for assets, called the **Asset Store**. It is a continuously growing store of Unity-specific content, ranging from single models or textures, to complete projects, but also extensions of the Unity software itself. Prices vary, but considering the effort of creating good and re-usable assets, they are very reasonable (sometimes even free) and can be real timesavers.

You can browse the **Asset Store** online (`https://www.assetstore.unity3d.com`) or inside the Unity GUI, through the **Asset Store** tab by navigating to **Window** | **Asset Store**. You need to register with Unity to be able to download packages from the **Asset Store**. Downloaded assets are stored locally on your machine and you can import them in other projects too. Be sure to read the documentation per package, as there may be some particular constraints or license limitations.

Lightmapping packages in the Asset Store

If you want to take the Lightmapping process a bit further, the following are some additional tools in the **Asset Store** you might wish to try out:

- *Lightmap Manager Lite* is a free extension which gives more control over the Lightmapping process, including resizing and even blending Lightmaps, available at `https://www.assetstore.unity3d.com/#/content/342`.

- *Lightmapping Extended* is another free extension that enables all *Beast* Lightmapping settings and provides advanced configuration, available at `https://www.assetstore.unity3d.com/#/content/6071`.

- The *LHGS Lighting System* is not free but it adds an additional rendering calculation to Unity, which can improve lighting and especially the ambient occlusion quality. This also works in Unity Free, available at `http://forum.unity3d.com/threads/182422-LHGS-Lighting-System-for-Unity-Indie?p=1246629` and can be purchased from: `https://www.assetstore.unity3d.com/#/content/8683`

Pre-rendered models

While Unity has a very well integrated Lightmapping system, it might make sense if you do the baking in dedicated rendering software, such as to use advanced *Global Illumination*. Most current DCC applications support light baking, including CINEMA 4D and 3ds Max.

When you use, for example CINEMA 4D, this is available for texture/light baking. This can be achieved by following these steps:

1. When a scene is set up, select the object and choose **Bake Object** from the **Objects** menu inside the **Objects** browser.

2. In the dialog, activate **Ambient Occlusion** and **Illuminate** and choose an output folder to save the textures to.

3. When you press **bake**, CINEMA 4D will render the lighting and materials onto the object and create a new mesh, with optimized UV mapping. The original mesh is kept hidden if you ever wanted to make any changes.

4. When the baking is done, check that it works, by disabling GI and lights and call render. In a fraction of a second, the model will be re-rendered.

5. When you load this model into Unity, ensure that you hide the original object and only retain the baked one. Beware that the material for the baked object has a black basic color set, which should actually be white, or the whole object turns out pitch black. Load the rendered and baked texture onto the object. Set the **Shader** to **Unlit/Texture** to only retain the color of the texture.

Limitations

This procedure mixes both texture maps and lighting, lowering the resolution of the maps considerably. There is also no integration with Unity lighting and shadows, so it is hard to mix regular and baked geometry. Many people rely fully on the integrated Lightmapping in Unity or bake the full scene in external software.

Alternatively, you can use a **Self-Illumin/Diffuse** shader, and use the Lightmap in the **Illumin (A)** map. Beware that you need to change the texture properties of that map to generate an **Alpha channel** from the grey-scale image, as the Illumin channel only takes the alpha channel into account (indicated by *A*). With such a setup, you get a slightly different result, which still integrates with Unity lighting and thus can cast and/or receive shadows.

The following screenshot shows two ways the baked material can be set up:

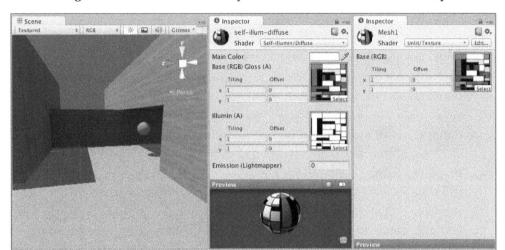

There is a nice video tutorial, which explains a more elaborate procedure step-by-step at the link http://www.youtube.com/watch?v=CsSxUSvdrgg. Two bake passes are performed in CINEMA 4D. The first one bakes the materials into a new texture map, as shown previously, while the second bake ensures all baked textures are now part of the regular diffuse material, avoiding the manual adjustments that were required.

For users of SketchUp, *LightUp* available at, http://www.light-up.co.uk) is an interesting solution. It provides light baking inside SketchUp and supports a real-time view inside the viewport. In addition, it adds FBX export (which was missing in the free edition of SketchUp). The baked lighting can be loaded as a Lightmap inside Unity. They provide an optimized shader and import script, to assist with the Unity setup.

Summary

This chapter took our starting scene a big step further. Lighting is essential in architectural visualization and Unity provides several options to tweak and improve the visual quality of your scene.

While you can get quite far with the free version, lighting with the pro-version is more advanced with Area lights, Bounced lighting, and Sky lights to improve Lightmapping results. In addition, the full screen image effects give a more polished effect to the result. Luckily for the users of the free version, real-time hard shadows were added for Directional lights in Unity 4.2, which could be used in any architectural scene. But use them sparingly, when you need interactive lights.

The next chapter looks at navigation in our project, using character controllers.

4
Promenade Architecturale

This chapter refines how you can set up basic navigation. While this will not explain how to create and rig characters, it will explain the use of the basic character controllers and how to set them up properly. We also discuss the use of camera objects, since it makes no sense to walk around a model without showing it.

In this chapter, we will cover:

- First Person versus Third Person Controller
- Loading a custom character from the **Asset Store**
- Using cameras for a minimap
- Display static text/information on screen

First Person versus Third Person Controller

In *Chapter 2, Quick Walk Around Your Design*, we explained how to load a default character controller, which is included with Unity. The behavior of character controllers is provided by script components. Normally, when you author a scene, you don't need to be concerned about the inner workings of the actual script. You merely assign variables and adjust parameters.

Many typical 3D action games use a first person perspective, where the camera is positioned to mimic the view through the characters own eyes. Sometimes, you also see your virtual hands or some kind of weapon, for example, **Splinter Cell**, **Far Cry**, or **Half-Life**. This is the recommended way to view an architectural model, as you can easily look around in all directions and it feels more immersive.

The alternative, which can be experienced in games such as **Tomb Raider**, **Grand Theft Auto**, or **Assassin's Creed**, is a third person perspective, usually showing the main character from slightly above and behind. The camera follows the character and is usually equipped with a spring-like motion, which eases the character movements a bit. If done right, it is good for getting more involved with the character. We'll compare both setups more in detail later in this chapter.

Setting up the First Person Controller

The **First Person Controller** (FPC) combines a **Graphics** and a **Main Camera** object. We already described how you could use the default FPC prefab in *Chapter 2*, *Quick Walk Around Your Design*. We will briefly explain how this setup works and how you can refine it.

As illustrated in *Chapter 2*, *Quick Walk Around Your Design*, the FPC contains three **GameObjects**. Firstly, the **First Person Controller** is an **Empty GameObject**, which contains most of the scripts and components required as follows:

- The **Character Controller** component is used to define the main parameters of the FPC and is used to refine movements. You can use the **Slope Limit** and **Step Offset** to set the steepest angle and highest step the controller can take. By default, this is **45** degrees and **0.4** units respectively.

- The **Mouse Look** script reacts to mouse movements left and right, defined by the **MouseX** value for the **Axes** parameter. This defines the direction in which the FPC will move.

- The **Character Motor** script steers the actual navigation movements. There are several parameters to refine, for example, the maximum movement speed, the availability of jumping, and how sliding and other movements are controlled.

- The **FPSInput** Controller script links keyboard presses and game controller movements (defined by the **Input Axes** in the script) with the **Character Motor**. Two keyboard setups are activated by default. The W - A - S - D keys, which form almost an arrow on QWERTY keyboards are common in games and indicate the direction in which the controller will move. However, they are not practical with Azerty or other keyboard layouts. The arrow keys are set up as an alternative control configuration and they are more universal, especially as most clients for architectural visualization projects are only casual gamers, at best.

Secondly, as a child of the **First Person Controller**, a **Graphics GameObject** is attached, which contains a capsule-shaped **Mesh** inside the **Mesh Filter**, using a **Capsule Collider** that prevents the player from walking through walls. The **Mesh Renderer** component of the **Graphics** object is actually irrelevant, as the player would normally not see itself. It has no scripts or additional functionality.

Finally, the **Main Camera** object, as a sibling to the **Graphics** objects, is used to look up or down, relative to the capsule, using the same **Mouse Look** script as mentioned previously, but configured for up-down mouse movements, set by the **MouseY** value of the **Axes** parameter.

Beware that exploring with the mouse is not at all intuitive for casual game users, so take care of finding out which setup is most appropriate for your project and provide a level of in-game documentation.

You can tweak several settings, such as **Max Forward Speed**, or allowed **Slope Limit**, but the defaults are usually good to get started.

If there was already another **Main Camera** in the scene, you can remove it, or at least disable its **Audio Listener**, according to the warning on the status bar and **Console** log. This can happen with multiple controllers or cameras.

Setting up the Third Person Controller

As an alternative controller setup, we will now configure a **Third Person Controller** (**3PC**) that looks at our main character from behind:

1. Remove the FPC and drag the **3rd Person Controller** prefab onto the scene. It has an almost similar setup as the FPC. There is a main object with several components and two child objects containing both a skeleton (**Bip001** and all underlying skeleton positions) and the Mesh of the **construction_worker** model as shown in the following screenshot. Ensure it is positioned above the floor (for example, set the **Transform** component's **Position Y** value to 1.1).

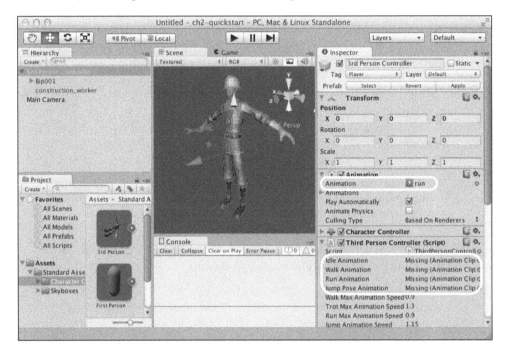

2. We had a few errors while running, so we fix them one by one:
   1. For some reason, the animations of the 3PC were not completely configured from the package by default, as visible in the previous screenshot of the first step. If you click on play, the character starts to run in place and continues to run the whole time, even while walking, waiting, and jumping, as the **Animation Clips** were not assigned properly. You can see the problems indicated as messages on the status bar and in the **Console** log. Messages are indicated by an exclamation mark and do not prevent the script from running, but are put there by the developer to log a certain message. Warnings and errors always indicate a problem that needs to be solved.

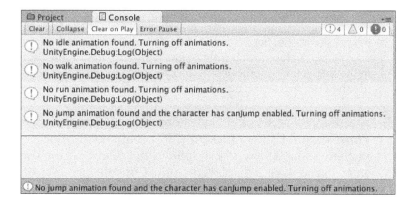

2. So how do we fix this? In the **Animation** component, the default animation refers to the **run** clip instead of **idle** clip, so the character will make the running movement the whole time. Moreover, the clips in the **Third Person Controller (Script)** are indicated as **Missing (Animation Clip)**. Click the small circle to select the correct ones. The following screenshot gives the correct assignments, indicated in bold:

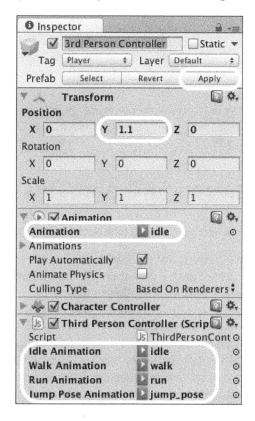

The bold text formatting means that these settings differ from the default settings in the loaded **Prefab**. You can turn them into the new default values, by clicking on the **Apply** button for the **Prefab** in the **Inspector**, as indicated in the previous screenshot. When you use the 3PC in other scenes, it will be set up from now on.

3. Additionally, you could have a problem with the camera setup. The **Third Person Camera (Script)** (TPC) component, attached to the 3PC, moves a camera around that follows the character. If it can't find it, an error message is displayed on the **Console** log. You can either assign any chosen camera yourself to the **Camera Transform** member variable of the TPC or rely on the built-in automatic lookup from the script. However, this requires a camera tagged as **MainCamera**, as shown in the following screenshot:

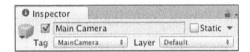

Tags are strings of text that can be assigned to a **GameObject**. They can be used for anything, but each object can only have one tag. In the example, a **MainCamera** tag should be available and assigned to the camera. The actual name of the camera does not matter here.

3. If you click on play now, you can navigate the **Worker** character around the scene. The character can be steered using the arrow keys. To have him jump up, use the space key.

Choosing between FPC and TPC?

Depending on your audience, one of the two navigation schemes might seem more appropriate, but that is something you have to decide for yourself.

For an inexperienced game author, the worker model from the TPC looks more user friendly and even "spectacular" if you are not into gaming and character modeling, but it is sometimes hard to steer this model through a small corridor or up a staircase. Moreover, as it is a default model, to simply illustrate what Unity can do, the cartoon-style of the construction worker is not really appropriate in a professional architectural visualization and his navigation is quite rough. We will illustrate a more extensive solution in one of the next sections and advice you to do this additional effort for more professional results. The default control system and especially the camera control are also not really suitable to allow the user to properly see the environment, which is the primary focus in architectural visualization.

The FPC is easy to set up, is less obtrusive, and provides a complete, immersive look on the scene, which puts the user in a visitor's viewpoint. However, to navigate a character by turning the mouse around needs some getting used to, certainly for inexperienced users, as the whole viewpoint is shifted around continuously. Some people even become seasick from such movements. Ensure you inform your user how this works, to avoid any bad experiences.

The 3PC is our personal favorite, if you replace the character with a more suitable one. Advanced game authors could even write scripts that allow the user to switch between both schemes, if required.

Further tweaking and refining the character controllers

Setting up a character controller, be it a FPC or 3PC, is often a matter of balance between semi-realistic and idealized navigation. In most cases, the character controllers move faster than in reality and take steeper slopes and higher steps than a normal person would. This is acceptable if you want the visual impression and spatiality of the design to be explored and not get bored by long running and walking times. Most game characters never get tired and can run and jump at all times. They even resurrect after they fall to death.

Running speed, **Step size**, and **Maximal Slope Angle** are the most important parameters you need to consider. Also take care of setting an adequate **Collider** size for the character controller. While game environments often feature big hallways, wide corridors, and vast terrains, architectural models are usually quite narrow. Doors might even be too small to navigate the character through. Some people re-scale the whole scene a bit, for better navigation. Consider expanding the viewing angle a bit, to show more of the interior.

A limitation of the default Worker model and the **Third Person Camera**, which steers the camera, is how you look around. Unlike the FPC, you cannot use the mouse to look up or down. To compensate a bit, you could limit the **Height** of the **Third Person Camera** script, to not look down too much, as indicated in following screenshot:

If you want to provide additional control over the viewpoint using the mouse, you could alternatively use the **Mouse Orbit** script from the **Scripts** package (**Assets | Import Package | Scripts**). This ensures that mouse movements are used to orbit around a particular target, so you can look around freely.

1. Create a new camera and attach the **Mouse Orbit** script onto it. Ensure its **Depth** is larger (For example, Depth = 1) than the **Depth** of the **Main Camera**, but don't remove this camera, as the 3PC script still needs it.

2. Set the **Target** parameter by dragging the 3PC onto the parameter value in the **Inspector** tab. This becomes the center for the camera to orbit around.

3. Adjust the **Distance** parameter of the **Mouse Orbit** script to **2** units, so it stays fairly close to the 3PC.

4. Set the **YMin Limit** and **YMax Limit** to **-20** and **80** respectively, which define the range of up and down movements.

A second alternative setup is re-using the **Mouse Look** script, which was already loaded from the **Character Controller** package:

1. Create a new camera and add it as a child of the **Main Camera**, so it follows its movements. Again, ensure **Depth** is set high enough.

2. Attach the **Mouse Look** script to this new camera and set the **Axes** to **MouseY**, so only up-down movements are allowed.

3. You could lower the **Sensitivity Y** to **5**, for slower movements and adjust the **Minimum Y** and **Maximum Y** to, for example, **-20** and **45** respectively to define the range of the movement.

Complete out-of-the-box solutions are available in the **Asset Store**, for example, the **KGFCameraSystem**, which presents several camera setups oriented towards architectural and product visualization (`https://www.assetstore.unity3d.com/#/content/6867`). There is an example, which temporarily orbits the camera around a 3PC while holding the right-mouse button. This is a valid way to combine an automatic camera with orbiting.

Getting camera behavior correct is an important aspect of presenting your design. If not properly used, the 3PC can be an unsatisfying experience for the (casual) user.

Loading a custom third person character

When you first start using Unity, you might be glad that there is a default character available. The **Construction Worker** model however, is a bit too cartoon-like and probably not generic enough for serious architectural visualization.

While it is possible to model a 3D character in software such as CINEMA 4D or 3ds Max, and animate using the character tools, this subject would easily take a whole book, yet still only touch on the most essential aspects. It is out of the scope of this book, so we will fall back on using stock models.

Using a custom static model

If you don't really need animations, your first option is to replace the worker model with a mesh of your own, which can be imported from any 3D modeling software.

Setting up realistic navigational constraints makes sense when you need to evaluate a design for people with limited navigation abilities. If you need to present an elderly care center, or a hospital, or any accessible building, it can be valuable to use a wheelchair simulation. This can be as simple as loading a custom character model, seated in a basic wheelchair and refining the controller movements and constraints. You need to limit the maximal slope angle, the step size height, the navigation speed, and the width of the **Capsule Collider**.

Loading a new character from the Asset Store

A good place to look for complete characters that work with Unity is the **Asset Store**. We will load one of the (few) free characters into our project and adjust it to re-use the default 3PC scripts provided in Unity as follows:

1. Go to the **Asset Store** and import the free **Max Adventure Model** (`https://www.assetstore.unity3d.com/#/content/3012`). Max is meant for a game, so he does not wear a business suit, but a backpack and black gloves. When loading animated meshes in a project, they get set up with a **Skinned Mesh Renderer** component, indicating that animations steer the character skeleton and deform the mesh (for example, legs that can bend). The **Animation** component is already loaded with the included animations, such as **walk**, **jump**, and **idle** (standing still, but with small, subtle movements). But apart from playing the default **Idle Animation** clip, Max will not walk around when you click on play.

2. Add the **Character Motor (Component | Character | Character Motor)**, which adds two components. The **Character Controller** component reacts when the arrow keys and space bar are pressed. It also has a **Collider Capsule**, which is not linked to a realistic physics simulation, but it calculates collisions to not walk through walls or fall through floors.

3. Adjust the **Capsule** position with the **Y**-value of the **Center** attribute, or Max will probably fall through the floor. The **Character Motor (Script)** is used to react on, for example, moving platforms. However, Max is still not set up yet to walk around.

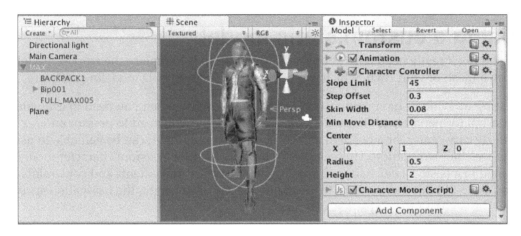

4. Add the **Third Person Controller (Component | Scripts | Third Person Controller)** where we need to link the correct animations included with the Max model to the different animation clip parameters of the script: **idle**, **walk**, **run**, and **jump** as shown in the following screenshot. The other parameters are for fine-tuning the timing. At this point, you can walk around with Max and he'll move as well. But our camera is standing still.

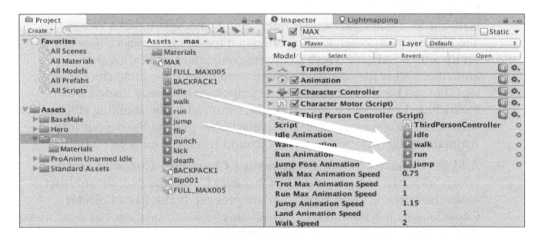

5. The final step is adding the **Third Person Camera (Component | Scripts | Third Person Camera)**, so the existing camera (with **Tag: MainCamera**) will follow him around.

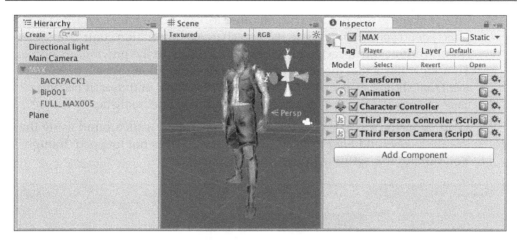

There are other models available (free or to buy), but you have to be careful as many characters only work with their own animation files.

Using Mixamo characters and animations

Mixamo is a company, which specializes in animated characters for different software systems. They have a complete library of characters and animations that is fully integrated with Unity. It is actually a store inside the **Asset Store**. You can browse models and animations and buy them directly from inside Unity. We will illustrate this with a package of free characters and one basic package of everyday movements, which could be all you need in an architectural visualization; that is, unless you want your own variant of Lara Croft who can climb, and jump, and rope swing, but there are packages for that too. The following steps explain how to retrieve a new Mixamo character with related movements from the Asset Store:

1. Download the freely available **Male Character Pack** from the **Asset Store** (`https://www.assetstore.unity3d.com/#/content/124`), which contains three low-resolution meshes of male figures. There is a similar `Female Character Pack` and one with Zombies (!). They do not contain any animations, however.

2. Also download or import the free **Mixamo Animation Store** package (`https://www.assetstore.unity3d.com/#/content/362`). This is used to order new characters or animations. If you look for animations, you won't find a complete set of suitable ones for free, unless you like Zombie walks.

3. We opt for **$30 Men's Everyday Motions "Unity4 Ready"**, which contains **Justin** (from the free Male Character package), with ten basic animations (`https://www.assetstore.unity3d.com/#/content/129`).

4. This package is compatible with all other Mixamo characters, which is a plus. Their system comes with its own character animation controller system (**RootMotionController**), which works differently to the previous examples. They steer the actual movement based on the animations, which prevents feet from sliding. Especially for the non-professional end user, it becomes easier to mix animations and characters and they look realistic.

5. Load the demo scene, which is set up to have **Justin** walk around using the *W - A - D* keys and *Shift* to start running. The *S* key is not mapped, though. You can use this setup with the other characters too.

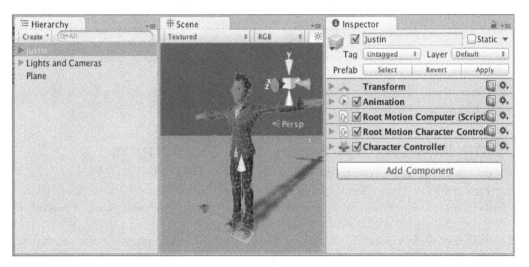

6. Try pressing the different numeric keys (for example, *1*, *2*, *3*, and so on) to see **Justin** laughing, waving, and jogging. Use *W - A - D* to switch back to regular movements.

To recreate this setup for your own scenes, carry out the following steps:

1. Add the default **Character Controller** component, the **Root Motion Computer** script and the **Root Motion Character Control** script to the top level **GameObject**, called **Justin**.

2. Add all provided animations that are included in the package to the **Animation** component of **Justin**, with the **Default** set to one of the idle animations (for example, *weight shift idle*).

3. Do not forget to add a **Third Person Camera** as well, if you need the camera to follow your character around.

As we preferred to steer this character using arrow keys as well, we altered a few lines inside the provided `RootMotionCharacterControlMENS` script. Inside the `Update` method, the different animations are prepared and linked to keyboard shortcuts. Unfortunately, as this script is part of the non-free Mixamo package, it cannot be shared, but the changes are minimal. Replace `Input.GetKey(KeyCode.A)` with `Input.GetAxis("Horizontal")>0`, `Input.GetKey(KeyCode.D)` with `Input.GetAxis("Horizontal")<0`, `Input.GetKey(KeyCode.W)` with `Input.GetAxis("Vertical")>0` but skip `Input.GetKeyDown(...)`. This way, not only the *W - A - D* keys are supported, but also the arrows. More information on the **InputManager** and the configuration of the **Axes** can be found on `http://docs.unity3d.com/Documentation/Components/class-InputManager.html`, where we also learn that, at least for the Desktop applications, these keyboard shortcuts are configurable by the user.

There are several other animation systems, which can be used to integrate moving characters inside Unity, such as 3ds Max, Maya, CINEMA 4D, and Blender. There are also some dedicated character animation systems, such as MotionBuilder, Poser, or Animeeple. But as previously mentioned, this is such a huge topic, that you could fill a whole new book with it.

Adding a live minimap

Many shooting games provide a radar-view on screen. This is an overview of the map, usually with some indication of enemies or targets. In an architectural context, you can add a minimap. This is a separate camera-view, in overlay on top of the regular view. You can either have a single broad view showing the whole scene or a smaller section, following the main navigation. While not immediately obvious, you can have multiple cameras at the same time. Each camera takes a part of the screen. The default camera uses the full screen. We will now show you how to add a second camera, that floats in front of the rest of the scene:

1. Create a new camera (**GameObject** | **Create Other** | **Camera**).

2. Set its **Camera** component to display an **Orthographic** projection rather than **Perspective**, which makes sense for a top view. This removes any perspective view distortion.

3. To look from above, set the **Transform** component **Position** to, for example, **X** = 0.0, **Y** = 5.0, and **Z** = 0.0. By setting the **Rotation X** = 9 0, you look downward.

4. The **Normalized View Port Rect** section is where you set the display size on screen, expressed as numbers between 0 and 1, indicating a percentage of the screen size (which is equal to the logical coordinates). In the example, we used **X** = 0.78 and **Y** = 0.75 to define the upper left corner of the view and **W** = 0.2 and **H** = 0.2 to define width and height respectively.

5. Optionally remove all other components (**GUILayer**, **Flare Layer**, and **Audio Listener**) as we are not using them here.

6. Set the **Clear Flags** field of the **Camera** component to **Depth only**. This ensures that everything that isn't seen by the camera stays transparent. Otherwise, you'd see the background color on that camera.

7. Be sure to set the **Depth** higher than the **Depth** of the **Main Camera** component. This forces the view from this camera to be shown on top of the other one, which is set to 0 by default.

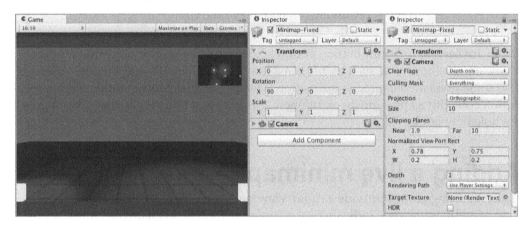

An alternative setup, that makes sense when using a **Third Person Controller**, is an isometric view that follows the main character, looking from above. The movement can be scripted or you can simply place the minimap camera as a child of the character.

Switching between cameras?

However, while the setup of the different cameras can be done with default Unity functions, you need a script to control switching. In its simplest form, enable/disable cameras or change their **Depth** value. A smoother approach is using an in-between camera that interpolates between positions. We will revise this idea in *Chapter 7, Full Control with Scripting*.

Setting up a turntable camera animation

As an example of a custom animation, we can use the same setup as shown for the Sun Study in *Chapter 3, Let There be Light*. To pivot a camera around the project—turntable style—you don't need scripting. Make an empty **GameObject**, add the **Camera** as a child, move it to the desired XYZ position and create an **Animation Clip** in which you animate the **Y**-rotation linearly from **0** to **360** degrees.

Displaying basic text/information on the screen

When giving feedback to the user, you can display text or images on screen. They are often placed as an overlay on top of the rest of the scene.

1. The simplest, but static approach is using a **GUITexture** or **GUIText** (**GameObject** | **Create Other** | **GUI Text** or **GUI Texture**), as shown in the following screenshot:

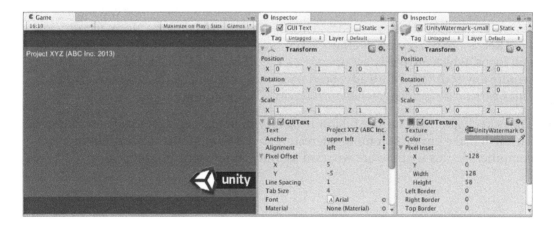

2. The **Transform** component works a bit differently from regular 3D positioning. They are expressed in **Screen** space, with **X** going horizontal from 0 (left) to 1 (right), and **Y** vertical from 0 (below) to 1 (top). Place the text at 5 pixels from the **upper left** corner, by setting the **Transform** position to **X** = 0, **Y** = 1 and the **Pixel Offset** in the **GUI Text** component at **X** = 5 and **Y** = -5.

3. To place a fixed image (for example, a Logo), follow the same approach: **Transform** position and **Pixel Inset**. The image should be loaded first as a 2D Texture (simply dragging any image into Unity suffices).

Beware that they are not the most efficient, performance-wise and you should limit their usage, especially on mobile setups. There are several GUI packages available in the **Asset Store** that optimize the amount of required screen calculations (*Draw Calls*):

- **NGUI** (`https://www.assetstore.unity3d.com/#/content/2413`) is a *Next-Gen UI*. It is a very popular user interface package, which ensures that the whole GUI will be drawn in a single screen update.
- **iGUI Basic** (`https://www.assetstore.unity3d.com/#/content/1946`) is a cheaper alternative, with a focus on WYSIWYG interface editing. If you need more features, there is also a more advanced version.

Summary

This chapter took control over navigation into the next level. We showed how to set up the **Third Person Controller** and how you can use either the default worker character or one of the **Asset Store** packages, which might come at a price. All setups, either FPC or 3PC also control the **Camera** component, which is essential to display anything on screen. Without a camera, you wouldn't see anything happening. But you don't have to stop at a single camera either. You can layer several cameras in the same scene, using the **Depth** field and the **Normalized View Port Rect** section. You can overlay even more information or simply add static text and logos, which are easily set up using a **GUI Text** and **GUI Texture**. They do not require any scripting. More advanced user interfaces will be discussed in *Chapter 7, Full Control with Scripting*, when introducing GUI scripting.

The next chapter will further fill our project with models and set up an environment. This will make our project more interesting, but also more demanding on the computer. So this is also were we need to think about scene optimizations.

5
Models and Environment

Most architectural photographs include furniture and props, to present the design in its full glory. To have a similar effect in our real-time project, we load additional models and set them up as properly scaled prefabs, which can be re-used throughout the project. We can place our project in a convincing environment, including terrain and sky.

After we have literally filled the scene with a large amount of objects, it is important to look at approaches to reduce the burden on the system.

This is again a chapter that is more reading and less doing. After all, optimizing performance is usually done by being clever and planning things properly.

In this chapter, we'll cover:

- Loading a model from the 3D Warehouse
- Setting up a basic landscape
- Creating a custom Skybox
- Working with large models

Loading 3D Warehouse models

To increase the impact of an interactive environment, it should contain sufficient detail. Furniture, accessories, plants, cars, and people can enliven the project. Rather than filling the model with every possible object, place some key items on visible locations around the scene. There are several online repositories of models, animations, and textures. The Unity **Asset Store** is an obvious entry, but do not underestimate the vast amount of online content that is freely available in **Trimble 3D Warehouse**. However, as the **terms of service** (**ToS**) are not fully clear for usage in commercial projects, you might want to rely on other sources or create your own models. You can either download models directly into Unity using the COLLADA format or prepare them first in other software. It is advised to start from the SketchUp model and at least clean up the normals (front/back faces), as explained in *Chapter 1, An Integrated Unity Workflow*, before exporting into Unity and properly assign materials and texture scale.

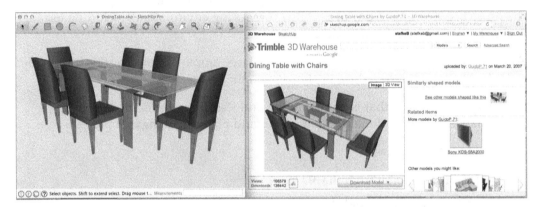

The download of a COLLADA file, with extension DAE, is usually a zipped folder, with some additional files for textures and an XML file for use with Google Earth. In fact, a KMZ file is the same thing. If you want to unpack the KMZ, rename the extension to ZIP.

When you drag or copy the file into Unity, the importer routine creates new materials for each found assigned material in the model. It might be necessary to link the textures again to these materials, so look at the material names.

We often encounter the same problems as noted in *Chapter 1, An Integrated Unity Workflow* and *Chapter 2, Quick Walk Around Your Design*: scale, wrong face normal, and non-optimized geometry. We usually scale the model with factor 0.1 or 0.01, but when it still looks off-scale, try 2.54 (or 0.0254), for example, when it was made in imperial units (feet, inch). As always ensure the scale is right on the importer settings.

Setting up a basic landscape

There are multiple approaches to add landscapes in an interactive scene:

- Unity has a dedicated **Terrain** tool, which is easy to get started with. A terrain is a large subdivided plane, where vertices can be lifted in the **Y**-direction: a so-called height field. While it takes a lot of effort to fine-tune to perfection, it provides the following interesting features:

  ° You can paint the height using brushes

  ° You can also paint the materials using texture maps

  ° You can add accessories, such as trees, bushes, and grass, which can move, as if the wind was blowing them

- When you already have a grey-scale height-image for your terrain, maybe made in Photoshop or containing real-world geography data, you can import this as a raw image. Refer to the documentation on: http://docs.unity3d.com/Documentation/Components/terrain-Height.html.

- If you created the terrain already inside your 3D environment, it can be loaded as a Mesh, just like any other imported Mesh. However, a regular mesh cannot be combined with the features of the Unity **Terrain** module.

- It is possible, with some effort, to turn a terrain from Google Earth into a Unity terrain. The process is documented by artist *3D Nemo* on: http://www.3dnemo.com/031_G_to_U.html. A terrain mesh is loaded inside SketchUp and the terrain textures are assembled in a Photoshop image. The final step, for which a script is provided, makes a Unity terrain, by sampling the height from the mesh. This is interesting, since copying the reference mesh into a real terrain can use all native Unity terrain features.

When you just want to add a basic model, you can import it as a mesh, but do not expect things to move or be interactive. For that, the Unity terrain is more suited. Due to space constraints, we refer to the online documentation and other books that go into detail on this, which are available from: http://docs.unity3d.com/Documentation/Manual/Terrains.html.

Customizing trees with Tree Creator

While initial versions of Unity came with example trees, there is a dedicated **Tree** tool, which has been included since Unity 4x. It allows users to build up a generated tree from branches and leaves, with several parameters controlling the generated 3D **Mesh**. To know more about the **Tree** tool refer the online documentation at: http://docs.unity3d.com/Documentation/Components/class-Tree.html.

To get started, load the **Tree Creator** package that comes with Unity (**Assets | Import Package | Tree Creator**). Start a new **Tree** object (**GameObject | Create Other | Tree**) and select the **Tree** component. Here you can fine-tune the geometry generation parameters.

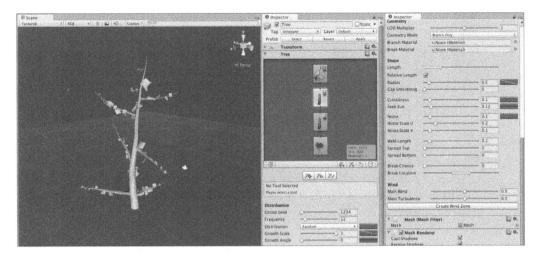

The **Tree** component displays the tree as a hierarchy of nodes. Start from below, with the main tree node and add branch and leaf groups. Each group is tied to its parent and controls parameters, for example, **Frequency** sets the amount of branches and **Length** sets the lengths.

To make the tree visually pleasing, you need to add materials too. The **Tree Creator** package includes examples to be used. Create a new material and use the **Nature/ Tree Creator Bark** shader. Add at least a base texture, for example, BigTree_bark_diffuse for the **Base (RGB) Alpha (A)** and **Gloss (A)** map and BigTree_bark_normal for the **Normalmap**. You need to assign this material to the **Branch Material** property on each relevant branch group. For leaves, a similar default is included.

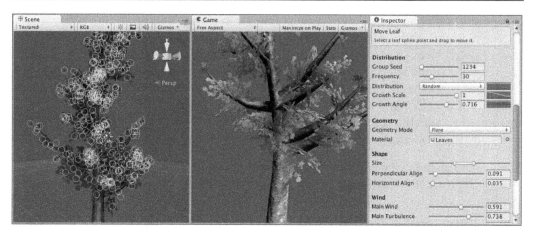

In the background, Unity generates optimized textures in a subfolder called `Treename_ Textures`, if you were wondering where these additional folders come from.

There is a lot more to it, for example, using **Curves** to fine-tune branch distribution and setting up the possibility of branches that break. Play with it, as the process is fairly intuitive, once you get the hang of the material system.

And finally, when you create trees, they can be integrated in the **Terrain** module too.

Creating a custom Skybox

When you want to include a credible environment, you can use the **Skybox** tool. This looks like a large cube, with seamless texture maps of skies placed on the inner side. By setting it around the scene, it follows camera movements and appears as if the whole sky surrounds your scene. There is a default package included with Unity that you can use (**Assets | Import Package | Skyboxes**) that contains about nine examples. A **Skybox** can be activated in two places, as shown in the following screenshot. You can activate a default **Skybox** material in the render settings (**Edit | Render Settings**). You can also define a **Skybox** material for a particular camera, by adding the **Skybox** component to it (**Component | Rendering | Skybox**).

It is possible to create your own **Skybox** images in almost any rendering software. Define a camera and position it perfectly horizontal. Set its viewing angle at **90** degrees. Record a six frame animation, with the camera orientated to one of the six cardinal directions in each consecutive frame. Unity presents the following shader slots, so it is best to stick to this particular order: **Front (+Z)**, **Back (-Z)**, **Left (+X)**, **Right (-X)**, **Up (+Y)**, and **Down (-Z)**. Render the animation as separate, square images and name them accordingly. This will render in just a few seconds, especially when the scene is empty.

Back in Unity, make a new material and use the **RenderFX | Skybox Shader**. Assign the correct textures to the slots and your material is ready. For slightly faster performance, you can also use **Mobile | Skybox**. Set the texture **Wrap Mode** to **Clamp** instead of **Repeat**, to avoid a nasty seam, which would spoil the effect.

If you have a panoramic rendering mode that supports **Cubic** projection, the camera setup becomes a one-click process, apart from cutting up the images and renaming them properly, a short six-frame animation is almost as fast to set up.

Optimizing scenes and models

While the performance of Unity running on current generation computers and handheld devices is still increasing, there are limitations to the amount of geometry you can place in an interactive scene. Especially trees, cars, curved models, and other objects with many polygons slow down Unity, sometimes dramatically. The following screenshot shows how to activate the **Stats** button on the **Game** view, which gives some insight in how much work Unity has to do.

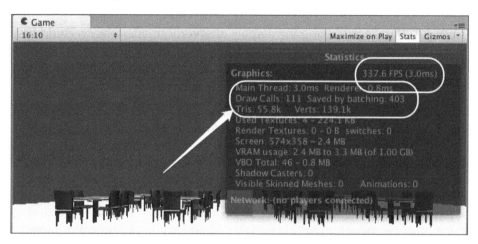

We try to reach at least 30 **frames per second (FPS)** for smooth display. In practice, we hope to attain 60 or more and drop down to 30 as a worst-case scenario. However, don't be too fixated on this number, as it is not an exact prediction of how the application itself will run, for example, on a tablet or in the Web Player. The Unity Wiki provides a utility script for that purpose. For more information on FPS visit: http://wiki.unity3d.com/index.php?title=FramesPerSecond.

Luckily, Unity itself does some optimization automatically. The Unity documentation provides some pointers to optimize performance. This documentation can be found at http://docs.unity3d.com/Documentation/Manual/OptimizingGraphicsPerformance.html, and you can go through some of the techniques, which help you getting Unity running smoothly (or less jaggy, at least). If you have a pro-license, the **Profiler** module gives a very detailed insight into the performance and possible bottlenecks.

While many of these optimizations are optional, whenever you target mobile users, or not this can mean the difference between success and failure.

Showing only what is needed

If you look directly to a forest, Unity needs to display all the trees, branches, and leaves. If you turn your head, there is no need to draw anything. Unity automatically applies so called **Frustum Culling**, which omits any object that falls outside the viewing frustum (a truncated pyramidal cone) of the camera. However, even if you see only a small fragment of a large object, it will be calculated as long as it is on screen. Frustum Culling happens for the whole object at once. It is therefore best to split and re-organize your model so any geometry that falls off screen can be omitted.

That said, the effort of preparing the display of several smaller objects could be significant. So avoiding geometry is a two-fold effort. Split your scene in multiple objects that can be culled automatically, but group nearby objects that are to be visible together.

Avoid loading model geometry that is never shown. If you run through a building, but only the lobby and a meeting room is open for visitors, there is no need to include other rooms, furniture, and installation systems. There is a reason why old games have loading screens and you often switch levels when you enter a building. It is possible to have one scene with only the exterior and the main building as merely a shell. When you enter the building, a script could unload the exterior and load the interior of that particular building. Clever use of fake geometry, such as pictures behind open windows, could be enough to get the feeling you are still in a larger environment.

The same technique can also be used to display design alternatives. There are a few approaches you can follow. You can decide to make each alternative a separate level. This is easy to set up, requires only minimal scripting (basically a one-liner call to `Application.LoadLevel(string levelName)`) and is by default optimized per scene. If you want to load alternatives on and off, you can decide on toggling visibilities, again using a simple script, or use an asynchronous loading of scenes, for example, load the content of one scene, while retaining the basics from your current scene, such as player and terrain.

The *Chapter 7, Full Control with Scripting*, will show you how to handle such tasks more easily.

Grouping objects by material

Whenever an object has to be drawn on the screen, it needs to be processed and translated into pixels. In any graphics engine, the system is switching all the time between different states. First you load a particular material and then you display geometry that gets this material applied. The more you need to switch, the more time it takes. Each separate material requires an additional draw call. So, combining objects that have the same material will speed up the display.

However, this might counter the effect we tried to get by splitting up the model into smaller pieces to be culled. Having many materials and using large objects will increase the amount of required Draw Calls, sometimes dramatically.

Using Prefabs (instancing)

If objects are repeated, instancing increases productivity and ease of scene organization. For example, if a model inside SketchUp is created using **Components** instead of **Groups**, they arrive as real instances, sharing meshes between instances, which can decrease the demand on the system. Having multiple copies of the geometry in a single file is more demanding than having multiple instances of the same, shared geometry.

In Unity, instances are called **Prefabs** and they can be created from any group of **GameObjects** that are placed in the scene. You create a new **Prefab** in the **Project** tab and drag a single **GameObject** onto it. If you need more objects, place them underneath an empty **GameObject** first. Prefabs are indicated by a blue name, instead of the default black one. They retain their scripts and other components as well.

- One behavior of Prefabs that might not be that obvious is that even though they share their definition, they can have their attributes set individually.

- A second characteristic is that Prefabs are stored as assets in the `Project` folder, which makes them easily re-usable across scenes. Should you want to transfer them to other projects, copy the assets or export them as a Package.

Luckily, every external model that is loaded is already a Prefab.

That said, the use of Prefabs will not reduce the effort of displaying them on screen: the same amount of geometry and materials takes the same amount of graphics processing, Prefabs or not. But do use the technique, as it will improve project organization and handling changes.

Using Levels of Detail (LOD)

This is a Pro Only feature, which allows automatic switching between different versions of a mesh, depending on the distance from the camera. While convenient, most CAD or BIM models are not created several times. However, with BIM software, you can create Views for different scale levels and switch between them in your project. You can get more information on LOD at: `http://docs.unity3d.com/Documentation/Manual/LevelOfDetail.html`.

If you don't have a pro-license, you could write a small script that calculates the distance from the Main Camera and accordingly hides or displays different versions of a model.

Culling and Batching

The objects that fall outside of the camera's viewing frustum are automatically skipped (Culling), as they are not visible for the user. Unity Pro provides the **Occlusion Culling** module, which is an additional step to indicate which objects are seen and which can be safely hidden. This requires an additional **Occlusion Culling** bake step.

So what is Batching? As an automatic aid to increase and optimize performance, Unity shifts your scene around at runtime, trying to call more objects in a single draw call, without any user interference. This occurs at runtime, after the visibility or culling calculations. There are two types of batching:

- **Dynamic batching**: It is used for moving objects that use the same material and are not affected by real-time shadows. This is automatic.

- **Static batching**: It is only available in Unity Pro and increases the efficiency of mesh rendering, by grouping meshes by material and other properties, to minimize draw calls. This is steered by indicating objects with the static attribute, just like we did when **Lightmapping** in *Chapter 3*, *Let There be Light*. No further intervention is required, but the effect is ignored in Unity Free.

You can get more information on Draw Call Batching at:
`http://docs.unity3d.com/Documentation/Manual/DrawCallBatching.html`.

Combining Meshes/Children

Remember the discussion in *Chapter 2*, *Quick Walk Around Your Design*, about a feature inside CINEMA 4D to reorganize the scene? Something similar is available inside Unity, called `CombineMeshes`, which groups geometry according to the used material. However, while this can indeed reduce draw calls, it can cause new problems, when approaching the limit of about 65.000 vertices per object and also because frustum calling is not as effective anymore with such large objects.

The `CombineMeshes` tool is available from a script that can be installed from the **Scripts** Package (**Assets | Import Package | Scripts**). Ensure that you load both **Combine Children** and **Mesh CombineUtility** from the `Utility Scripts` folder. These scripts are an alternative to the static batching optimization technique and work without a pro-license!

Select the object in the scene you want to optimize and call the script from the menu (**Component | Mesh | Combine Children**), which adds the script to the selected object. Nothing appears to happen, until the moment you click on play. The effect is only available at runtime! If you check the **Hierarchy** tab, shown in the following screenshot, your original model is reorganized by merging all geometry that was assigned the same material. You see a combined mesh per material with the original mesh renderers toggled off. When you stop execution of the game, everything turns back to normal.

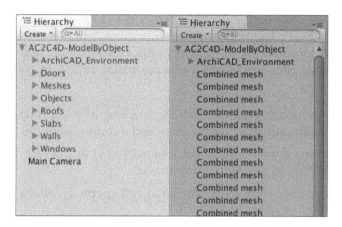

An improved version of this script, called `CombineChildren_962.cs` can be downloaded from the Unity forum: `http://forum.unity3d.com/threads/37721-Combine-Children-Extented-(sources-to-share)`. Rename it as `CombineChildren.cs` and remove the original one, before you can use it. This script exposes additional parameters and is more optimized.

There are some limitations with this approach, however. It takes additional computation at the start of your game and if you try to combine this script with **Lightmapping**, it fails. When the meshes are reorganized at runtime, the second layer of UV2 maps is not correctly recalculated. So while you might assume that the light maps were baked correctly inside the editor, they are removed again at runtime. In a discussion with one of our former students, *Thomas Van Bouwel* (`http://tvb-design.com`), he showed us a slightly adapted version of this script (available with this book), which recalculates the UV2 coordinates using `Unwrapping.GenerateSecondaryUVSet(...)`.

How does it work? Add the script to your parent object. By default, the script acts at runtime. This is fine as long as you don't need Lightmapping. Otherwise, right-click on the component and call the **Combine Now** context menu. This performs the combining directly inside the editor. This is also useful to inspect what the script would do at runtime. You can always revert back to the original model, as loaded models are prefabs. Remember to remove the script or at least disable it, so the UV2 generation is not called again in your final build. Otherwise, the lightmaps will not fit the model anymore.

We performed a few tests on the ArchiCAD model in *Chapter 2, Quick Walk Around Your Design*. It has 55.000 triangles and 71.200 vertices, which is not that much. FPS seems to fluctuate considerably in the Unity editor and the only real performance is what you get in an application running on a particular device. In general, we can see the following effects:

- The original model required 72 draw calls and 1070 additional ones that were saved by automatic batching. We reached a comfortable 130 FPS.

- Static batching lowered the amount of calls to 41 at 220 FPS. Use it if you have Unity Pro, as the effect is imminent.

- The CombineChildren scripts (original and adapted) reduce this to 37 calls (no batching), at about 94 FPS.

- After using the script in the editor (Combine Now), **Lightmapping** on the generated meshes results in the same amount of draw calls, but increased FPS (back to about 130) and made the shadows visible.

- In comparison, adding real-time hard shadows has a huge impact. When added to the original model, we need more than 3500 calls without batching and 2500 calls with batching enabled. The amount of geometry that is getting calculated as a result of adding shadows increased as well, to 174.000 triangles and 228.000 vertices. We hardly reached 40 FPS.

Your mileage may vary, as such optimization is highly dependent on the scene, but we have at least a few operations that we can apply on the model to increase performance.

Combining materials (texture atlas)

An additional optimization, which can further increase performance and one which is used widely in game authoring, is creating a texture atlas. Instead of using many different texture maps, they are combined in one or more assembly maps. This requires setting up the geometry with suitable texture coordinates. While it looks similar to Lightmapping at first sight, there is a huge difference: each part of the combined texture can be used repeatedly on different objects.

While most architectural models do not apply this technique, it can be partly automated. Read about it in the discussion of the *Bob script*, which is slightly dated but freely available from `http://forum.unity3d.com/threads/88604-One-draw-call-for-each-shader-with-dynamic-meshes-The-Bob-script`. The author improved this afterwards and it is now available from the **Asset Store** as the **Batching Tools**: `http://ippomed.com/unity/batching-tools-draw-call-batching-for-unity-3d/` and `http://forum.unity3d.com/threads/113508-Batching-Tools`.

An alternative system, also on the **Asset Store**, is the **Mesh Baker** package that helps to combine meshes and material. The creation of texture atlases is included as well in this package (`https://www.assetstore.unity3d.com/#/content/5017`).

Avoiding excessive collision geometry

You might remember when we imported FBX models in *Chapter 2, Quick Walk Around Your Design,* that we activated the **Generate Colliders** option in the FBXImporter Settings. A **Mesh Collider** is actually a copy of the geometry to be used for collision detection. This is fine and really handy, but it introduces some additional processing at runtime. Whenever the character is walking around or objects are being moved with the physics system, collisions are being calculated. This comes at a performance cost.

The first and obvious solution is disabling the **Mesh Collider** objects that you will not access, for example, the walls on the third floor for a closed building, the rooftops, and the surrounding buildings on other sites.

However, you need them on all objects on which you allow the character to walk. To increase performance, you could replace the **Mesh Collider** with a more simple shape. The **Box**, **Sphere**, and **Capsule Colliders** are much easier, as they are convex, rather than concave objects, and have fewer triangles to calculate.

Other examples are replacing a set of chairs and table with a single box, or replacing trees, plants, traffic signs, lamp posts, and other small objects with **Capsules**.

There are no real shortcuts here, but to dive in and painstakingly replace whatever geometry that can be simplified with these colliders. Remember that the meshes themselves stay visible, but the simplified colliders are used for physics and collision calculations.

Summary

While this chapter required more reading than doing, it contains several pointers to procedures to improve your project. We can load additional geometry, to enliven the scene. You can even add detailed terrains and trees and a nice sky image.

However, this all comes at a price; that is, performance may suffer. So the last few sections looked at several approaches to lower draw calls and increase the amount of frames we can display per second. It is also obvious that a pro-license simplifies many of these optimization techniques, but with some experience and a few helper scripts, there is a lot you can improve using the free version as well.

Get ready for our next chapter, on further improving the use of textures and shaders.

6

Shaders and Textures

When loading CAD or BIM models, geometry usually receives a basic color and in many cases a texture map. However, for convincing visual results, you need to fine tune the shaders and set up materials that are a bit more advanced. This includes applying different texture channels and using the shading power inside your graphics card (GPU).

In this chapter, we will cover:

- Basic textured materials
- Advanced textured materials
- Procedural materials
- Further material techniques

Adjusting basic textured materials

As we have already seen in the previous chapters, Unity adds materials for all applied textures and colors in imported models. However, as the materials defined in CAD or BIM exports tend to be fairly basic, Unity has little information to define a dull color and texture map, using the default diffuse shader.

 Every material in Unity is controlled by a "Shader". This is a series of instructions, written in an interpreted language that gets compiled into GPU instructions. Common shaders use textures, for example, color and/or bump mapping.

The first thing to do is to check the imported materials to ensure all textures are really defined and found. Ensure imported models have integrated UV coordinates to define how the texture is mapped onto the geometry. If you use different textures, you might need to adapt the scaling (tiling). Since materials are shared between objects, this affects all objects that reference the same material.

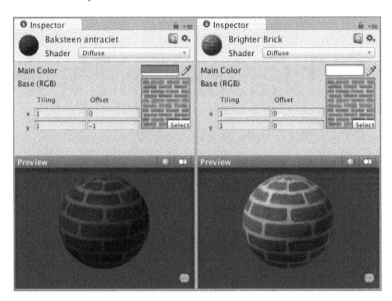

The **Diffuse** shader only has a **Main Color** and **Base (RGB)** map. The **Main Color** mapping modulates the material, so you can increase brightness simply by setting this color to white.

When switching to a **Diffuse Bump** shader option, you can additionally set **NormalMap**. In regular bump maps, each pixel's brightness indicates high or low bumps. With normal maps, an RGB color represents a normal vector (R=X, G=Y, B=Z). This gives more detail about the direction of the bumps and is directly supported by the GPU. If you don't use a suitable normal map, Unity displays a warning, **This texture is not marked as a normal map**. By clicking on **Fix Now**, as shown in the following screenshot, Unity adapts the image import settings to generate a suitable normal map. However, please do this for a copy of the image file, as the same file cannot be a regular texture and normal map at the same time:

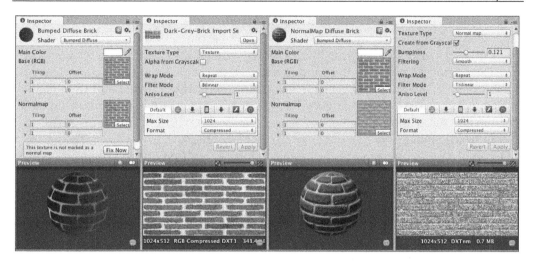

In the example, we copied the original texture and inverted the image, as the mortar lines were bright, which indicates that they lie above the darker regions. When setting as **Normal map**, we enabled **Create from Grayscale**, indicating that only brightness values are taken into account. The **Filtering** option was set to **Smooth** instead of **Sharp**. Click on **Apply**.

This approach can be followed for most building materials that are not transparent or reflective, such as concrete, wood, bricks, and soil.

Creating convincing glass

A very basic, elementary glass material can be simulated using the **Transparent/Specular** shader, available by default. It has support for both the **Main Color** and a **Specular Color** map. In the following screenshot, we set the **Main Color** option to transparent, by adjusting the alpha component (A) to be below 255.

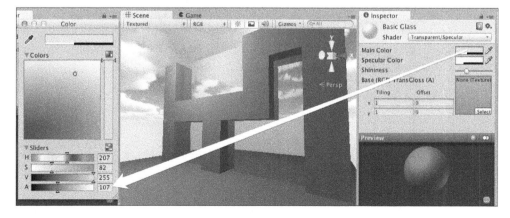

Even though this provides a fast transparent material, it is not convincing. While full ray traced reflections will take some more years to become viable in real time systems, there are tricks to at least give the illusion of reflectivity. The same way a Skybox was simulated using a CubeMap, this kind of map is also usable to fake reflection. There is a series of reflective shaders in Unity (for example, **Reflective/Specular**), but they do not provide support for transparency. Luckily, others have provided a suitable shader that can be used without much effort. Two suitable glass shaders are documented on the Unity wiki (`http://wiki.unity3d.com/index.php/Glass_Shader`). The basic **Glass** shader is very simple and looks a bit similar to our first attempt done previously, so we will use only the second, more advanced example, called **Glass Reflective**. This uses a CubeMap to fake reflections from the environment. While not really reflecting the scene, it provides a convincing effect in a real time environment when you use the same CubeMap as your Skybox material. We will now illustrate how to apply the example glass shader code in your Unity project:

1. Start a new shader (by navigating to **Assets | Create | Shader**) and double-click on it to open the default code editor (**Monodevelop**, usually, if you allowed it to be installed with Unity initially).

2. Although this is not a complete overview of shading programming, we explain this example in detail to understand what is going on. Luckily, the first section is simple, as it only defines the basic name and sets properties to be available in the **Inspector** tab and their default values:

```
Shader "Glass Reflective" {
Properties {
  _SpecColor ("Specular Color", Color) = (0.5, 0.5, 0.5, 1)
  _Shininess ("Shininess", Range (0.01, 1)) = 0.078125
  _ReflectColor ("Reflection Color", Color) = (1,1,1,0.5)
  _Cube("Reflection Cubemap",Cube) = "black"{TexGen CubeReflect}
}
```

3. In the following code, we indicate that this is a transparent material. This is rendered after the opaque objects are rendered to blend the colors.

```
SubShader {
  Tags {
    "Queue"="Transparent"
    "IgnoreProjector"="True"
    "RenderType"="Transparent"
  }
  LOD 300
```

4. In the shader program (CGPROGRAM) the actual calculations are coded. The color sampled from the CubeMap (reflcol) is first modulated (multiplied) with the RGB channel of the reflection color (_ReflectColor.rgb) as set previously. This defines the output emission (o.Emission). The same reflection color is also multiplied with the alpha channel of the reflection color to set the output opacity (o.Alpha). The output (o) is what is returned back from the shader to the graphics system. The shader program is as follows:

```
CGPROGRAM
    #pragma surface surf BlinnPhong decal:add nolightmap
    samplerCUBE _Cube;
    fixed4 _ReflectColor;
    half _Shininess;
    struct Input {
      float3 worldRefl;
    };
    void surf (Input IN, inout SurfaceOutput o) {
      o.Albedo = 0;
      o.Gloss = 1;
      o.Specular = _Shininess;
      fixed4 reflcol = texCUBE (_Cube, IN.worldRefl);
      o.Emission = reflcol.rgb * _ReflectColor.rgb;
      o.Alpha = reflcol.a * _ReflectColor.a;
    }
  ENDCG
}
```

5. And finally, the Fallback section ensures that the shader will render at least something when the GPU cannot render the preceding instructions. You see this with most shaders. The Fallback section is as follows:

```
FallBack "Transparent/VertexLit"
}
```

6. Ensure that your glass material uses this shader. Assign the material to geometry or adjust the existing (imported) material from your CAD or BIM model to use this shader, so that it is applied throughout the scene at once.

In the following screenshot, the example on the left uses the basic **Glass** shader (for which we did not show the code), whereas the **Glass Reflective** example to the right adds **Reflection CubeMap** (for example, one of the Sky maps from the Skybox package).

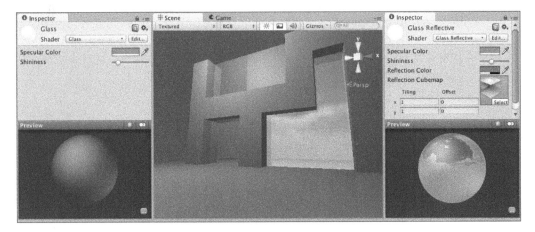

 Beware that the example uses a single plane object, which can only be seen from the front side. If you need the effect from both directions, add back-faces.

The preceding example works fine, but for more complex reflective glass, you need a pro-license, which performs a separate rendering pass from the camera and projects the mirrored scene onto the material at the cost of longer rendering times.

Using advanced textured materials

While you can go pretty far using the Unity shading language, we will focus on the use of image-based texture maps mostly in architectural visualization. We illustrate this with textures from the Arroway website (http://www.arroway-textures. com/catalog), which are provided commercially in high resolution or can be freely downloaded in low resolution, under a Creative-Commons license (CC-BY, so attribution is required if you apply them in your projects).

1. Go to the Arroway website and browse to a texture that you like. We opt for **bricks 002**, which gives a nice weathered brick pattern. You get a preview of how the texture looks when applied to an example.

2. Note the hints that are provided here: real world size is **6m x 3.4m** and the texture is seamless only in the horizontal direction, so you should not repeat it in the upper direction. Download the RAR archive and unpack it. It contains three files: `bricks-002_b030.jpg` is **bump map**, hinted at **30%** intensity, `bricks-002_d100.jpg` is **diffuse map**, to be used at **100%** intensity, and `bricks-002_s100-g100.jpg` can be used as specular and/or gloss map, depending on the software you use. While the image is only 864 by 463 pixels in size, this is still a fairly usable resolution for renderings and more than enough for a real time model:

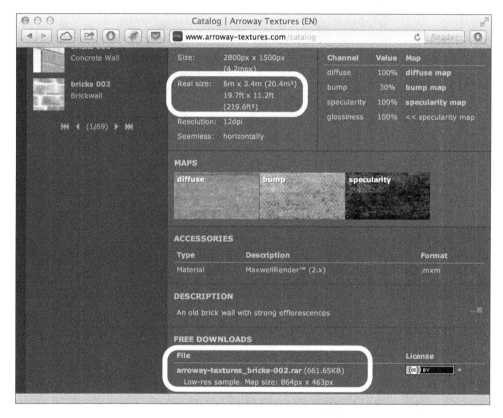

3. To try it out, create a cube in Unity with scale **X=6**, **Y=3.4**, **Z=0.2** and position **Y=1.7** to place it just on top of the ground floor.

4. Create a new material and name it `bricks-002`. Instead of the default diffuse shader, switch to a **Bumped Diffuse** or a **Bumped Specular shader**.

5. Now you can drag the diffuse map (`bricks-002_d100`) to the **Base (RGB) Gloss (A)** texture slot. The RGB color channels are used as the main color.

6. You need an alpha channel to be able to change the glossiness. You currently don't have one, as this is not supported with JPEG files. You can use Photoshop to create a new PSD file using the diffuse map as RGB channels and the specular map (bricks-002_s100-g100) as the alpha channel.

7. As a quick alternative, you can select the diffuse map in Unity and check the **Alpha from Grayscale** option in the **Inspector** window, which at least does something that is a bit similar to a real gloss map. Be aware that the specular maps are created for this exact purpose, so they provide better results.

8. Drag the bump map (bricks-002_b030) to the **Normalmap** slot and don't forget to turn it into a real normal map by clicking on **Fix now**.

9. Select the bump map and adjust its settings in the Inspector window as shown in the following screenshot. Set **Bumpiness** to a fairly low value (**0.04** or so), and **Filtering** to **Smooth,** or else the effect will be too exaggerated and quite ugly.

If you need to integrate this with your CAD or BIM system, it is best to configure the textures directly inside your master model by performing the following steps:

1. Edit one of the applied materials to use the downloaded diffuse texture map and set the correct real world scaling as noted previously. This ensures that the exported model has proper texture positioning, so we can replace them with more advanced textures in Unity.

2. Load the project in Unity and look for the generated material. It will already have the basic diffuse shader, although sometimes you need to manually add the texture map again.

3. Now you can switch to a more advanced shader and assign a normal map and optionally a specular or gloss map. Since this material definition is shared between objects, it gets replaced in the whole project at once.

Using procedural materials

Although it is not currently common in CAD or BIM software, most DCC applications not only support colors and textures, but also procedural materials using some kind of shading language. Shading languages can be very extensive and support many other instructions. Current GPUs calculate advanced shaders in real time. The glass shader above is a basic example of a procedural shader.

Allegorithmic substances

As we don't expect our readers to simply start writing such shaders, and this book has no room to discuss them either, we suggest an alternative route and use a procedural shading system that is more directly accessible for end users.

Allegorithmic is a company that develops a procedural material system called "Substances". They have an authoring environment where you can create new materials and they even sell individual materials. Many 3D systems, including Unity, support substance shaders. In the Asset Store, check the *8 FREE Substances for Mobile* package (`https://www.assetstore.unity3d.com/#/content/1352`), which illustrates the potential of these materials. Although they increase the loading time of scenes, they take few resources, so the resulting files are really small when compared with comparable regular textures. They look quite detailed even when zoomed in, and they are compatible with the supported mobile platforms as well. The following screenshot illustrates the available **Procedural Properties** and the generated texture images:

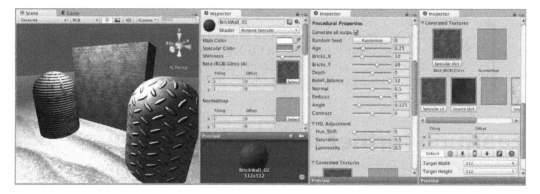

Installed Substances come in packages, with embedded materials and textures. Fold out the shader package icon in the **Project** tab and drag the underlying Substance material onto an object, as shown in the following screenshot. You can tweak many settings, so a single material can actually have multiple variants with widely differing results. In the background, the procedural system generates regular texture maps that are applied without any additional user intervention.

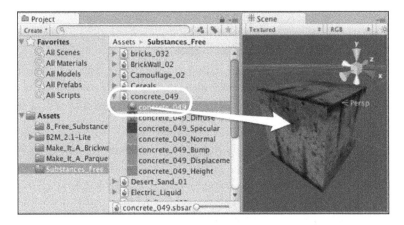

With *Bitmap2Material*, you can generate a complete shader, including diffuse, specular and bump maps, based on a single image. It even has options to remove tiling, to make the texture seamless, to remove lighting, and to even out shading. Check out the free watermarked Lite version at:
`https://www.assetstore.unity3d.com/#/content/5687`.

> On www.crazybump.com, you can also download a free demo application for Windows and OS X that does something similar, by generating normal maps from regular images. The final normal map can be used directly inside Unity.

Learning further material techniques

While the majority of texture work was explained previously, there are some additional techniques that you can apply in your projects.

Adjusting texture mapping

When materials are defined, you set up characteristics that are often defined by textures (images). However, the material only defines the look and not how the actual textures are placed on the geometry. This is done at the modeling stage (for example, inside your 3D, CAD, or BIM software). The latest architectural authoring software provides textures as part of the material properties and allows you to define the real size of a texture map; for example, inside the ArchiCAD material editor, you can define the visual properties of a material, including setting the real world size of a texture as follows:

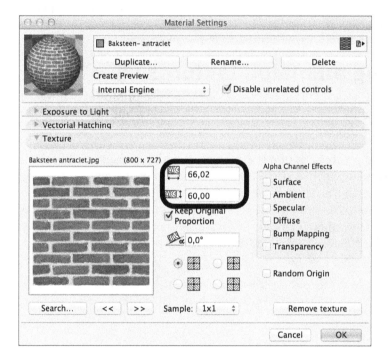

If you modify a material to contain another texture, be sure also to adapt the real world size of the texture map immediately, so that it will be positioned at the right scale.

When you export your model into Unity, the texture (as part of the material) stays at the same place. The projection of the texture map onto the model gets stored inside an additional set of coordinates per vertex, called the "UV" coordinates, as opposed to the XYZ coordinates defining the vertex position in a Cartesian coordinate system.

 Correct texture mapping in the model, before exporting it to Unity.

When you replace a texture with another that does not conform to the same size, you need to adjust the tiling of the material. This will change the appearance of this material on all places where it is used and this is not always what you want. Moreover, if your 3D model only contains solid color information, no texture coordinates are assigned and Unity has no way to link a texture to the geometry.

 Always assign textured materials on your geometry, even just as placeholders, before exporting to Unity.

Unity is not a complete model and texture authoring tool, but is an environment where all these are assembled.

Applying animated textures

Unity supports animated materials through the use of Movietextures, which can be used for animated television screens or other effects, but they require a pro-license and have some limitations on a mobile platform.

If your animation consists of a few frames, it makes sense to apply the technique of sprites. This is similar to a small cartoon movie or an animated GIF. There are (quite) a few packages in the Asset store, as they are widely used for 2D games, but you can create your own sprite manager with some scripting. You either have a series of separate images that get switched or a single image with multiple sections where you adjust the offset to switch to the next frame of the animation.

At the time of writing of this book, Unity announced that a sprite management system would be available with the release of Unity 4.3.

Summary

We discussed mainly the use of textures to assign visual properties to materials. For architectural visualization, this is good to emulate bricks, concrete, metal, and wood. To display a convincing glass, we used a custom (copied) shader. And finally, we illustrated procedural textures.

The final chapter will go into scripting and we introduce a few reusable scripts that can be used to further tweak and control what we learned throughout the previous chapters.

7
Full Control with Scripting

Architects often express that they are visual artists and not programmers. While you can get reasonably far without resorting to scripting, it's almost impossible to finish a project that way. This chapter presents a few easy and reusable scripts that can be applied in most projects. This chapter is enough to get you started. We advise you to type all examples from scratch. It'll take a bit longer and you may encounter errors. It is easier to elaborate something you wrote and understand, than it is to extend somebody else's code.

In this chapter, we will discuss:

- Scripting crash course
- Triggering doors and elevators
- Basic heads-up-display with a custom GUI to toggle objects or display info
- Switching between cameras and materials
- Further interactions: resetting the player, loading other scenes/levels

Scripting crash course

Right now, you already used scripts. They are at the heart of Unity. To add behaviors to objects, Unity uses components. If you need lighting behavior, add a `Light` component. If you need physics behavior, add a `RigidBody` component. If you need custom behavior, add a `Script` component.

A script has particular entry points, which define the flow of execution. Some functions are automatically called when the game runs, others every time the display is refreshed, possibly several hundred times per second. You enter the code into one of these functions or call custom functions from these entry points. In the background, scripts are compiled and bundled into your final application, so they run as fast as built-in functions and behaviors.

Internally, Unity uses the *Mono framework*, an Open Source implementation of the *.NET framework*, which was designed and developed by Microsoft as a modern and extensible framework. It works independently from the high level programming code the programmer writes, and supports multiple platforms, including not only Windows, OSX, and Linux, but also Android and iOS. While Unity supports JavaScript, C# and the aptly called *boo*, in practice most people use JavaScript or C#,. If you have a background in Web development, the *UnityScript* version of JavaScript is the easiest to get into. On the other hand, C# is more akin to C++ or Java and is the best starting point if you have some programming experience. Since custom development for CAD and BIM applications relies on such languages and since many Unity developers embrace C#, we will use this for the rest of the chapter. Luckily, scripts are easily ported between these languages and you can mix and match scripts using all supported languages.

 Some of the scripts in this section are based on examples generously provided by Pieter Jorissen and Ivan De Boi, from the Karel de Grote Hogeschool (University College) in Antwerp (Belgium).

Triggering doors and elevators

We will now write a simple script that is directly applicable in our example project and extend it afterwards to be more generic and reusable, using parameters.

Doors and elevators are typical interactive elements in buildings. Most buildings have no other moving parts. To rotate a door manually or to use scripting is not that different. However, there are a few tricks to get it correct. These are as follows:

1. Create a plane GameObject, positioned in the origin. Add a simple Cube, and name it DoorLeaf. Set its position to **X**=1, **Y**=1.5, **Z**=0 and scale to **X**=2, **Y**=3, **Z**=0.1. This ensures that the lower side corner of the door leaf is sitting in the center or our scene.

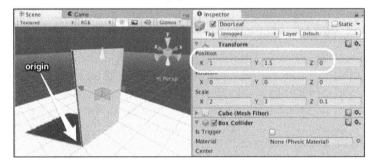

2. Load the local documentation from the menu by navigating to **Help |
   Scripting Reference**, which opens your default browser on the starting
   page of the locally installed Unity documentation, which is also accessible
   offline. On the first page there is a small menu to choose the language of
   all examples (JavaScript, C# or Boo).

3. Type `rotation` in the search field to get a list of entries on rotation.

4. Click on **Transform.rotation**, which directs you to the documentation of
   the rotation property of the Transform component. You can get and set
   this property using `transform.rotation`.

5. Switch back to Unity, create a new C# script by navigating to **Assets |
   Create | C# Script**, and name it `rotateObject`.

6. If you double-click on the script name in the Assets tab, Unity will launch
   the default code editor, which is **MonoDevelop** with most installations.

> MonoDevelop is an Open Source editor targeted at Mono development,
> but it can be used for all scripting languages inside Unity. It is a
> complete **Integrated Development Environment (IDE)** with syntax
> coloring, code-completion, search and replace facilities, line numbering,
> and even full debugging support. Refrain from using a basic text editor
> such as Notepad in Windows or TextEdit in OSX. In Windows, many
> C# developers also use Microsoft Visual Studio.

Inside MonoDevelop, you get a template script, which does nothing at the moment,
but is set up to start entering code.

The first two statements load the main Unity class library and the Mono/.NET
collection classes that are needed to work with lists of objects. These statements
are given as follows:

```
using UnityEngine;
using System.Collections;
```

Downloading the example code

You can download the example code files for all Packt Publishing books
you have purchased from your account at http://www.packtpub.
com. If you purchased this book elsewhere, you can visit http://
www.packtpub.com/support and register to have the files e-mailed
directly to you.

Next up is the class definition, which derives from MonoBehaviour (the mother class for all Unity scripts). As a convention, the class name should be identical to the script name (without the file extension .cs). Unity will complain otherwise. This is shown in the following statement of code:

```
public class rotateObject : MonoBehaviour {
```

Variables and classes are declared between curly brackets. The Start() method gets called just once when the script launches (usually when you press play). The void qualifier indicates that the method or function will not return a value or variable upon use. This is shown in the following piece of code:

```
// Use this for initialization
void Start () {

}
```

The Update() method is called continuously, whenever a frame in the game is updated. This is shown in the following piece of code:

```
// Update is called once per frame
void Update () {

}
```

Do not forget the final closing bracket to complete the class:

```
}
```

Now we can enter some new code to add some actual behavior to this class. Adjust the Update method by typing (and not copying) the following code:

```
void Update () {
   this.transform.rotation = Quaternion.Euler (0,90,0);
}
```

Unity uses *Quaternions* to indicate rotations. They are numerically more stable than vectors and don't lead to drifting when you continuously rotate entities. The Quaternion class has an Euler method to set the rotation using three values for X, Y, and Z, respectively. This is exactly what you would type inside the transform component fields. Set all three angles in one call when using Euler-angles. Contrary to many other programming environments, you don't need to convert angles from degrees to radians first. This is done as given in the following steps:

1. Drag this script onto the **DoorLeaf** object. It now has a component called **Rotate Object (Script)**, which is derived from the script and class name. Notice the capitalization and the space inside the name! It has one parameter, called **Script**, which is set to **rotateObject** (the name of our script).

2. Press play to see what happens. Press **stop** and play a few times to double check. The DoorLeaf rotates abruptly and stays in a rotation state while the script is running. It returns to its former position when you stop the script.

3. Okay… that's not really much, is it? Up to this point, our script is really simple and unusable, as the door is rotating around its center, rather than around a hinge. This can be set up with a proper GameObject hierarchy. To add the door hinge, create an empty GameObject by navigating to **GameObject | Create Empty** and name it Hinge. Set its position and rotation to **X**=0, **Y**=0, **Z**=0. It now sits in the corner of our door leaf.

4. Drag the door leaf onto the hinge object, to define a hierarchical relation, as shown below. Check the setup by manually changing the Y-rotation of the hinge. The leaf should follow along.

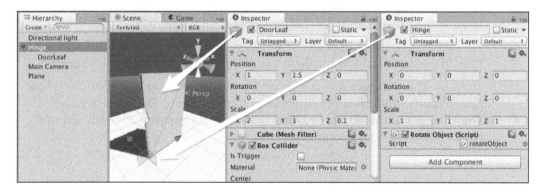

5. Adapt the setup by removing the script from the leaf and adding it to the hinge instead. Press play to see that the leaf rotates around the hinge.

If we would use `transform.Rotate()`, we'd get a different behavior. This command adds a rotation to the current rotation, whereas setting the rotation variable replaces it. For example, `transform.Rotate(0, 5, 0)`, when placed in the `Update` method, continuously adds a 5 degree rotation with each frame renewal.

Using triggers and colliders

The previous script is very basic. We set the rotation directly when the script starts. In most cases, we want to control when this occurs. Inside Unity, we receive a notice when objects collide. If you add a `Collider` component to any GameObject, it reacts when other objects bump onto it. The system calls the `OnCollisionEnter()` event to which we can react within our script. When set to `Trigger`, the `Collider` component works a bit differently. Triggers do not obstruct other objects, but detect when they enter their collision volume (often a box or sphere). We could use this to find out when our player enters a room (`OnTriggerEnter`) and when the player leaves again (`OnTriggerExit`). This is done as given in the following steps:

1. Add a Cube so it extends in front and behind the door leaf. For example, position **X**=1, **Y**=1.5, and **Z**=0 with scale **X**=2, **Y**=3, and **Z**=6. Name it `DoorTrigger`.

2. Since Cubes come with a `Box Collider` component automatically, we don't have to add one ourselves. Just ensure that you toggle its **Is Trigger** property, so the box will not obstruct the player.

3. Disable the **Mesh Renderer** component, to make it invisible.

4. Add an Empty object in position **X**=**Y**=**Z**=0 and name it `Door`. This will group the other elements. Leave scale at 1 or the children will behave erratically!

5. Drag the **DoorTrigger** and **Hinge** on **Door**, to make them a child. The whole group is now underneath a single object, called **Door**. Do not attach the **DoorTrigger** to the **Hinge** or **Door Leaf**, as the triggering zone should not rotate while the door is opening.

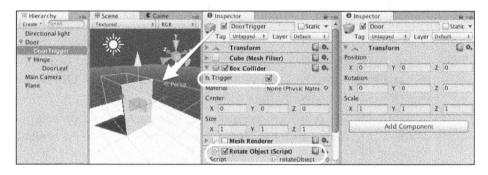

6. Remove the previous version of the **rotateObject** script, which was attached to the **Hinge** object. Use the script given as follows:

```
using UnityEngine;
using System.Collections;
public class rotateObject : MonoBehaviour {
```

Add two *public variables* to the script. `Target` can hold any GameObject from the scene. `Angle` is the amount of degrees we want our door to rotate. We write the angle as `90.0f` to indicate this is a `floating-point` number. Public variables become visible in the Inspector of the object with the script attached.

```
public GameObject Target;
public float Angle = 90.0f;
```

`Collider` objects that are set to `Trigger` call the `OnTriggerEnter` and `OnTriggerExit` events. We ignore the `Collider` parameter `other` for now, as shown in the following piece of code:

```
void OnTriggerEnter(Collider other) {
  Target.transform.rotation = Quaternion.Euler (0,Angle,0);
}
void OnTriggerExit(Collider other) {
  Target.transform.rotation = Quaternion.Euler (0,0,0);
}
} // closing bracket
```

You can remove the Start and Update methods completely, as they are not used here. This is done as shown in the following steps:

1. Now you can re-attach the script to the **DoorTrigger**. Drag the **Hinge** item in the **Hierarchy** tab onto the **Target** parameter slot of the **Rotate Object** script to assign the variable used by the script.

2. To finish off, add a first or third person controller into your scene and press play. Whenever you run into the **DoorTrigger** zone, the script gets called and the door should open, by rotating the **Hinge** and the attached **DoorLeaf**.

Refining the opening animation

While we now have a fully functional door, its animation is very crude and abrupt. We will use a technique called *easing* to smooth the door movement and make it more appealing. The trick is to set the angle not in single step, but gradually, each frame getting closer and closer.

Add three more variables to the script, but make them private, to not expose them to the user. They are used to set the angle we aim for (targetAngleY), the value it has at the moment (currentAngleY), and a small number to control how fast the angle will evolve towards the target value (easing), as shown in the following piece of code:

```
private float targetAngleY = 0.0f;
private float currentAngleY = 0.0f;
private float easing = 0.05f;
```

We move the rotation code to the Update() method, as it needs to be called on each frame. The current angle will be increased in gradual steps, by multiplying the difference between the target and the current values with the easing value, as shown in the following piece of code:

```
void Update() {
  currentAngleY += (targetAngleY-currentAngleY) * easing;
  Target.transform.rotation =
    Quaternion.Euler (0.0f, currentAngleY, 0.0f);
}
```

Now the two trigger methods are simply used to set the correct `current` and `target` values. The original public `Angle` value is never changed, so we can continue to open and close the door by running in and out of the trigger zone. This is done as shown in the following code:

```
void OnTriggerEnter(Collider other) {
  targetAngleY = Angle;
  currentAngleY = 0.0f;
}
void OnTriggerExit(Collider other) {
  currentAngleY = Angle;
  targetAngleY = 0.0f;
}
```

 Did you notice that these changes did not require another setup of the door hierarchy? Even with multiple copies of the door, they'd all use the same script.

Moving platforms

A very similar script can be used to define a sliding door or a moving platform, using translation instead of rotation. The sliding door is fairly trivial, but the moving platform will be problematic, at first. This is explained in the following steps:

1. First the setup. Add a cube to become the moving platform and name it `Platform`. Place it where you want and adjust its scale.

2. Add a second Cube called **Tower**, and adjust position and scale to become a place where you want the platform to arrive at the end of the translation.

3. Create a third Cube to act as a trigger and name it `PlatformTrigger`. Position and size it so it sits just above the platform, defining a zone to enter. Disable its **Mesh Renderer** and toggle the **Is Trigger** parameter, just like the previous example. Make it a child of the platform, so the trigger zone follows the platform. Your setup should resemble the following screenshot.

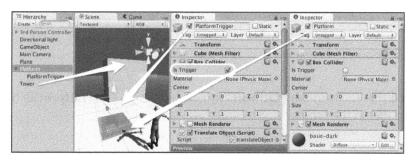

4. Now create a new C# script, name it `translateObject`, and add the following variables, just after the class declaration, as shown in the following code:

```
public Vector3 targetPosition;
public GameObject Target;
private Vector3 startPosition;
private Vector3 moveCurrent, moveTarget;
private float easing = 0.01f;
```

5. In the `Start()` method, we initialize our private parameters, so we retain the original position and set the current and target positions appropriately. This is shown in the following piece of code:

```
// Use this for initialization
void Start () {
  startPosition = Target.transform.position;
  moveCurrent = startPosition;
  moveTarget = startPosition;
}
```

6. The `Update()` method does the easing, but instead of using floating-point numbers, we calculate directly using vectors, since most useful methods are implemented in the `Vector3` class, such as addition, subtraction, and multiplication. This is shown in the following piece of code:

```
// Update is called once per frame
void Update () {
  moveCurrent = moveCurrent + (moveTarget-moveCurrent)*easing;
  Target.transform.position = moveCurrent;
}
```

7. Then the trigger methods do the trivial work of setting the `moveTarget` variable appropriately. Beware that this forces the platform to return to its original position when the player steps off. This is shown in the following piece of code:

```
void OnTriggerEnter(Collider other){
  moveTarget = targetPosition;
}
void OnTriggerExit(Collider other){
  moveTarget = startPosition;
}
```

8. Add this script to the **PlatformTrigger** and assign the **Platform** as the `Target` variable of the script.

9. Adjust the **Target Position** X, Y, and Z values to be somewhere where you want the platform to arrive. Did you notice that this reflects the `targetPosition` public variable, which was of type `Vector3`?

10. Press play and walk the player onto the platform, which should start translating. Observe what happens when the platform is moving forward.

Solving a problem with parenting

This setup has a very annoying problem! Whenever the platform is moved horizontally, the player gets left behind and falls off! While the vertical movement of the platform continuously triggers the player to detect the floor below, it does not detect any other movement. Luckily, the solution is fairly simple. We temporarily make the player a child of the moving platform. Just be sure to undo this when the player leaves the platform.

 When using the character motor form the FPC, the scripts take care of it.

1. The following `switchParent` script does just that. It first retrieves the player by searching for it using the **Player** *tag*. If you use the FPC, you need to add this tag manually. This is only done once, when the game starts. This is shown in the following piece of code:

```
using UnityEngine;
using System.Collections;
public class switchParent : MonoBehaviour {
  public GameObject newParent;
  private GameObject thePlayer;
  void Start () {
    thePlayer = GameObject.FindWithTag("Player");
  }
```

2. In the trigger methods, we set our player's `transform.parent` variable to be the transform component of the `newParent` variable. This is shown in the following piece of code:

```
  void OnTriggerEnter (Collider other) {
    thePlayer.transform.parent = newParent.transform;
  }
  void OnTriggerExit(Collider other) {
    thePlayer.transform.parent = null;
  }
} // closing bracket
```

3. Attach this script also to the **PlatformTrigger** and set the `newParent` variable to be the platform object.

4. Press play and walk the player onto the platform. It should follow the movement of the platform. Also check what happens in the Hierarchy tab when you leave the platform again.

Beware that these first few scripts lack error checking. We can compare the tag of the colliding object with the **Player** tag, to be certain that only the player will trigger the platform and not some other object flying or moving around.

```
void OnTriggerEnter (Collider other) {
  if (other.gameObject.CompareTag("Player"))
    thePlayer.transform.parent = newParent.transform;
}
```

Do the same in the `OnTriggerExit()` method.

Rework the script using an animation clip

We illustrated the use of animation clips in *Chapter 3*, *Let There be Light!*, with the Sun Study. There we created an animation clip that was played at the start of the game or level. However, you need a script to launch an animation clip at a particular event, such as when triggering.

```
using UnityEngine;
using System.Collections;
public class playAnimation : MonoBehaviour {
  public GameObject target;
  void OnTriggerEnter (Collider other) {
    if (other.gameObject.CompareTag("Player")) {
      target.animation.Play();
    }
  }
}
```

This is quite straightforward and works fine if your object has a single animation loaded that is set as default. It is also reusable, as you don't need to alter the script when using other animation clips. When you have multiple animations, you have to address the specific animation from the list. We set variables that require an animation clip to be assigned. The next example calls a clip when entering a trigger and another when leaving, as shown in the following piece of code:

```
using UnityEngine;
using System.Collections;
```

```
public class toggleAnimation : MonoBehaviour {
  public GameObject target;
  public string enterAni;
  public string exitAni;
  void OnTriggerEnter (Collider other) {
    target.animation.Play(enterAni);
  }
  void OnTriggerExit (Collider other) {
    target.animation.Play(exitAni);
  }
}
```

Here we use a string variable to set the animation clip name. This is really flexible, but you have to be careful not to type any mistakes.

 Always strive for reusable, generic scripts. Start small and limit scripts to one particular purpose. If you need multiple, unrelated behaviors, use different scripts. You can always attach more than one script to a GameObject.

Basic heads-up-display with a custom GUI

When we explained the use of GUIText and GUITexture components in *Chapter 4, Promenade Architecturale*, they were static. This is fine for a fixed logo, but not when you need dynamic information. You can script these components, but they are not the most efficient ones to use. This is shown in the following code:

```
public Texture2D someTexture;
...
guiText.text = "Hello";
guiTexture.texture = someTexture;
```

An alternative is the use of the Unity **Graphical User Interface (GUI)** classes. To display a GUI inside a script in Unity, use the OnGUI() event. This runs independently of the regular Update() cycle. Inside this event, you can display buttons, text labels, sliders, panels, scroll areas, textures, and toggle switches.

We illustrate this with a simple GUI script that displays the name of the trigger we enter, as shown in the following screenshot, which also displays some feedback in the console.

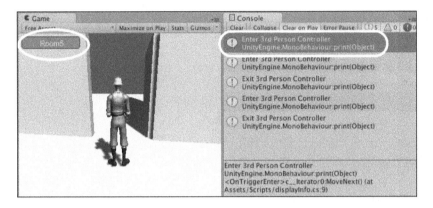

The following steps will show how to set up a simple scene with a few walls and floors:

1. Add a few Cubes and name them appropriately. Adjust their scale to cover the room volumes.

2. Set each `Box Collider` as a trigger and disable their Mesh Renderers, as in the following screenshot.

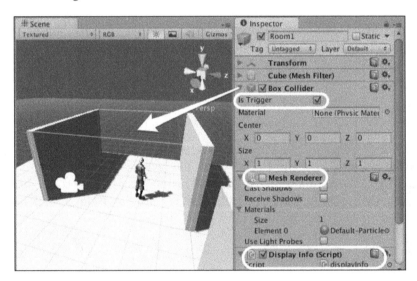

3. Create a C# script `displayInfo` to attach to each trigger, as shown in the previous screenshot.

4. Adjust the script to contain a private variable `display` to toggle the GUI.

```
using UnityEngine;
using System.Collections;
public class displayInfo : MonoBehaviour {
  private bool display = false;
```

5. The triggers toggle the `display` variable when entering and leaving. This is done as shown in the following code:

```
void OnTriggerEnter(Collider other) {
    if (other.gameObject.CompareTag("Player")) {
      display = true;
    }
  }
  void OnTriggerExit(Collider other) {
    if (other.gameObject.CompareTag("Player")) {
      display = false;
    }
  }
```

6. Finally, inside the `OnGUI()` method, we call the `GUI.Box()` method when needed. It displays the `name` of the GameObject inside a `GUI.Box` positioned 5 by 5 pixels from the top left corner and 100 by 20 pixels wide. This is done as shown in the following code:

```
void OnGUI(){
    if (display == true) {
      GUI.Box(new Rect(5,5,100,20), name);
    }
  }
} // closing bracket
```

There is a slight graphical problem. When you exit one volume that is adjacent to the next, both names overlap for a split second. Adding a slight delay or a fading effect masks this. The following alternative implementation of the `OnTriggerEnter()` method includes a *Coroutine* that instructs a delay of 1 second. Beware that in this case you need to change the `void` return type to `IEnumerator`. You cannot simply insert a pause inside the script, as the execution of the game would stop. Coroutine is a technique to execute scripts in parallel routines. For more info on the use of Coroutines visit: `http://docs.unity3d.com/Documentation/ScriptReference/Coroutine.html`

```
IEnumerator OnTriggerEnter(Collider other) {
   if (other.gameObject.CompareTag("Player")) {
     print("Enter " + other.gameObject.name);
     yield return new WaitForSeconds(1);
     display = true;
   }
}
```

Toggling lights and other objects

We introduced lights in *Chapter 3, Let There be Light!*. In a dynamic project, you could add light switches or change lighting scenarios. The next example displays check boxes on screen to toggle the visibility of preselected light and meshes. Create a C# script called `toggleObjects`, as shown in the following piece of code:

```
using UnityEngine;
using System.Collections;
public class toggleObjects : MonoBehaviour {
```

The script has a public variable named `objectList`, which is an `array` of `GameObjects`, as indicated by the square brackets. It can host any GameObject. To fill the array, drag the necessary objects from the Hierarchy tab onto the variable, which adds slots to the list. This is shown in the following code:

```
public GameObject[] objectList;
void OnGUI() {
  int index = 0;
```

A `foreach()` loop steps through the list one object at a time. In each loop step, we refer to that object using the `obj` variable (or any other name we decide to use for it). This is shown in the following code:

```
foreach ( GameObject obj in objectList){
```

Calculate the vertical on-screen position of the GUI element in the `posY` variable, in each step. When `index` increases, we move a bit further down. This is shown in the following code:

```
int posY = 5 + 20 * index;
```

If that object has a `renderer` component, add a Check box (`GUI.Toggle`) on screen and set it to reflect the current visibility, by asking the `enabled` state of the `renderer`. This is shown in the following code:

```
if (obj.renderer != null){
  obj.renderer.enabled =
    GUI.Toggle(new Rect(5,posY,140,20),
      obj.renderer.enabled, obj.name);
```

However, if it has a `light` component instead, use the `enabled` state of `light`. This is shown in the following code:

```
} else if (obj.light != null) {
  obj.light.enabled =
  GUI.Toggle(new Rect(5,posY,140,20),
    obj.light.enabled, obj.name);
}
```

Increase `index` at the end of the loop step, to move the next GUI element further down. This is shown in the following code:

```
        index++;
    }
}
```

This can be further refined, if needed, for example, to distinguish between more object types or when the object has both a Mesh Renderer and a Light component.

Another improvement is *recursive* toggling, to take child entities into account. This is shown in the following piece of code:

```
    void toggleRecursive(Transform element, bool toggle){
      if (element.renderer != null)
        element.renderer.enabled = toggle;
      foreach (Transform t in element.transform){
        if (t.renderer != null)
          t.renderer.enabled = toggle;
        toggleRecursive(t, toggle);
      }
    }
```

When calling this recursive function, use the `transform` property of the GameObject, because this is where the parent-child hierarchy is kept. We also check if the result of the `Toggle` is different from the current state of the `renderer` for that object, as shown in the following piece of code:

```
    if (obj.renderer != null){
      bool toggle = GUI.Toggle(new Rect(5,posY,140,20),
        obj.renderer.enabled, obj.name);
      if (obj.renderer.enabled != toggle)
        toggleRecursive(obj.transform, toggle);
    }
```

The result is seen in the following screenshot, with the script attached to the **Main Camera** (but it could be any other object). Several scene objects are added to the **Object List**. When running the game, the check boxes appear in the display and when clicked you see the Mesh Renderer or Light component being toggled in the Inspector.

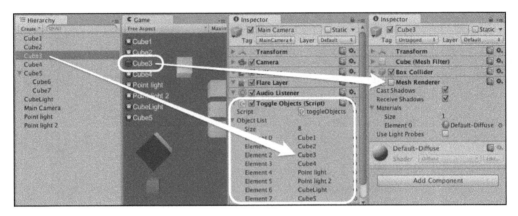

A good use case for such a script is when your design is comprised of several alternative parts. You can export all parts into your scene and use this script to display toggles for the individual sections of the building. The recursive method helps to toggle all elements in the underlying hierarchy.

Switching between cameras

While previous examples always used a single camera, apart from the mini-map, you can dynamically change cameras using scripts. You could modify their Depth parameters, so another camera is drawn above the others, but you could also toggle their state. In a more elaborate setup, you could switch between different cameras, for example from first person to third person perspective or to a dedicated **Point-of-View (POV)** camera to display a particular viewpoint. It is also a way to toggle between user-driven navigation and a pre-animated camera. The following steps show how to perform this:

1. Prepare your scene with a few camera objects created and positioned in different places. Ensure that only one camera has an active Audio Listener component, to avoid warnings in the console log.

2. Create a new C# script and name it switchCamera. Add a public variable, cameraList, to contain a list of available cameras, using an array. An index variable is used to keep track of which camera to enable. This is shown in the following piece of code:

```
using UnityEngine;
using System.Collections;
```

```
public class switchCamera : MonoBehaviour {
  public Camera[] cameraList;
  private int index = 0;
```

3. Within Start, step through the list of cameras with a foreach command to disable them one by one. Only enable the first one (indicated by index). This is shown in the following piece of code:

```
void Start () {
  foreach (Camera cam in cameraList){
    cam.enabled = false;
  }
  cameraList[index].enabled = true;
}
```

4. We don't need the Update() method, but there is no harm in leaving it in.

5. The OnGUI() method displays a button to toggle the next camera and disable the current one. To right-align the button, use Screen.width. This is shown in the following piece of code:

```
void OnGUI(){
  if (GUI.Button(new Rect
    (Screen.width - 105, 5,100, 20), "Next Camera")){
    cameraList[index].enabled = false;
    index = (index + 1) % cameraList.Length;
    cameraList[index].enabled = true;
  }
}
```

6. To use this script, attach it to an empty GameObject and fold out the **Camera List** parameter. Set its **Size** to the number of cameras you want to manage and drag your scene cameras into the slots that become available.

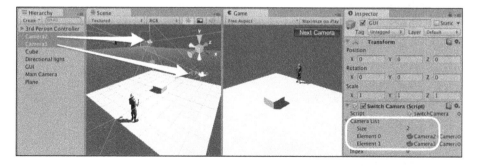

7. When you press play, a button is visible to toggle the active camera.

This script can be improved with *easing*. An additional `private` camera gets smoothly translated and rotated towards the position and rotation of the camera indicated by `index`. In this script (`switchCameraEasing`), all cameras in the list are actually toggled off. This is shown in the following piece of code:

```
using UnityEngine;
using System.Collections;
public class switchCameraEasing : MonoBehaviour {
  public Camera[] cameraList;
  public Camera   cameraMaster;
  private float easeSpeed = 0.125f;
  private int index = 0;
  void Start () {
    foreach (Camera cam in cameraList){
      cam.enabled = false;
    }
    cameraMaster.enabled = true;
  }
```

The easing occurs in the `Update()` method. Instead of the previous technique, we use the `Lerp` function, which stands for *Linear Interpolation*. This technique is shown in the following piece of code:

```
void Update () {
  cameraMaster.transform.position = Vector3.Lerp
    (cameraMaster.transform.position, cameraList
    [index].transform.position, easeSpeed);
  cameraMaster.transform.rotation = Quaternion.Lerp
    (cameraMaster.transform.localRotation, cameraList
    [index].transform.localRotation, easeSpeed);
}
```

Since we disabled all cameras initially and only move `cameraMaster` around, there is no need to further enable or disable other cameras. This is done in the following piece of code:

```
void OnGUI(){
  if (GUI.Button(new Rect (Screen.width - 105, 5,100, 20)
    , "Next Camera")){
    index = (index + 1) % cameraList.Length;
  }
}
} // closing bracket
```

If one of the cameras is the main camera from the Character Controller, you get errors in the console log when disabling it. Instead of toggling it completely off, you could lower the Depth parameter instead and keep it activated.

Switching between materials

An interesting interactive option you can provide to clients is choosing between different material finishes. A good example of such a system can be found in *Autodesk Showcase* at http://www.autodesk.com/products/showcase/overview, which displays a popup list of material thumbnails in a very realistic real-time view of a design.

We follow a similar approach as the camera switcher, by setting up a list of alternative textures and using the OnGUI() method to display a button to switch between alternative materials. It is important to prepare the list of textures on beforehand. This is shown in the following code:

```
using UnityEngine;
using System.Collections;
public class switchMaterials : MonoBehaviour {
  public Material[] materialList;
  public GameObject target;
  private int index = 0;
  void OnGUI(){
    if (GUI.Button(new Rect(5,5,100,24), "Next Material")){
      index = (index + 1) % materialList.Length;
        target.renderer.material = materialList[index];
    }
  }
}
```

Similar to the *Showcase* application, the GUI.Button() method supports textures instead of text. To retrieve the basic texture of a material, use the mainTexture variable, as shown in the following code:

```
void OnGUI(){
  int counter = 0;
  foreach (Material mat in materialList){
    int posY = 5 + 36*counter;
```

```
    if (GUI.Button(new Rect (5,posY,100,24),mat.mainTexture)){
      target.renderer.material = mat;
    }
    counter++;
  }
}
```

An alternative is to use the GUI.DrawTexture() method, which is not a button, but has more control over texture placement and scaling according to aspect ratio. This is done in the following statement:

```
GUI.DrawTexture(new Rect(5, posY, 100, 24)
  , mat.mainTexture, ScaleMode.ScaleToFit, true, 100.0f/24.0f);
```

You can place the texture thumbnail alongside or even behind the button. Best results are found when using textures of the same size and aspect ratio, so they also map correctly onto the object. Otherwise you also have to adjust UV-tiling of the affected material.

Further interactions

We finish this chapter with some more useful techniques.

Resetting the player

What if, at one point, the user reaches the edge of the terrain or world you created and falls off? Instead of expecting the user to quit and restart, you should solve the problem elegantly. We place a large, invisible plane underneath our world, as a trigger to reset the player.

1. Add a **Plane** GameObject and set its Mesh Collider to **Is Trigger**. Make it large enough to extend to all sides of the scene and move it down underneath all other objects, as in the setup in the next screenshot.

2. Disable its **Mesh Renderer**, to make it invisible.

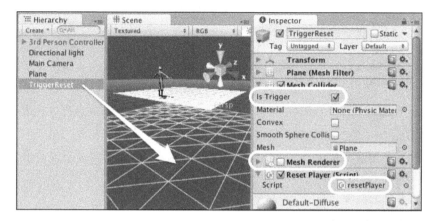

3. Create a new C# script called `resetPlayer` and add the following code. It takes three private variables: one for the player's position (`pos`), one for its rotation (`rot`), and then the actual reference to the player (`thePlayer`). This is shown in the following code:

```
using UnityEngine;
using System.Collections;
public class resetPlayer : MonoBehaviour {
   private Vector3 pos;
   private Quaternion rot;
   private GameObject thePlayer;
```

4. There is no need to set up anything when using this script, as we store the player's position and rotation directly at the start. We use the `GameObject.FindWithTag()` function. Just ensure the script is attached to an object with its `Collider` set as **Is Trigger**. This can be seen in the following code:

```
// Use this for initialization
void Start () {
   thePlayer = GameObject.FindWithTag("Player");
   pos = thePlayer.transform.position;
   rot = thePlayer.transform.rotation;
}
```

Here we check that the trigger only reacts to the Player. When hitting the trigger, we reset its position and rotation to the previously stored values `pos` and `rot`.

```
void OnTriggerEnter (Collider other) {
  if (other.gameObject.CompareTag("Player")) {
    thePlayer.transform.position = pos;
    thePlayer.transform.rotation = rot;
  }
 }
}
```

If your player is the 3 PC with a camera that smoothly follows along, you also get an animated camera transition with it.

Loading another level

Inside Unity, levels are organized across Scenes. You can use scenes as menus or as full levels. Before we can switch between Scenes, however, it is important to ensure they are added to the **Build Settings** by navigating to **File | Build Settings**. Here you can add all scenes you want to be included in your final application and you can also switch between the supported platforms, depending on your license.

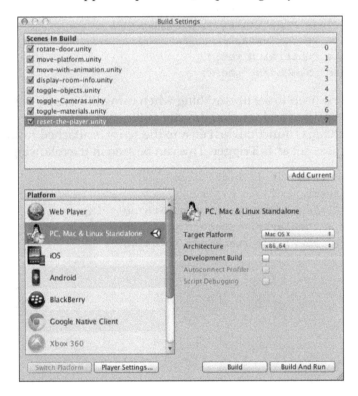

The next fragment loads a level using a `string`, but you could use an integer as well.

```
using UnityEngine;
using System.Collections;
public class loadLevel : MonoBehaviour {
  public string Level;
  void OnTriggerEnter (Collider other) {
    if (other.gameObject.CompareTag("Player")) {
      Application.LoadLevel(Level);
    }
  }
}
```

When you need to reload the current level, pass the name or index of the current level:

```
Application.LoadLevel(Application.loadedLevel);
```

Some additional Asset Store tips

It might feel strange to talk about "Scripting without scripting," but there are a few systems that help you generate scripts without having to actually write code yourself.

- *iTween* (`https://www.assetstore.unity3d.com/#/content/84`) is a free animation system to create smooth transitions between positions and other transformations, giving a pleasing, professional feel to animations.

- A companion system to iTween is the *Visual Editor for iTween*, which replaces writing code with a visual programming interface, available at: `https://www.assetstore.unity3d.com/#/content/180`

- Another visual programming system, which is even more extensive, is *uScript*, available at `https://www.assetstore.unity3d.com/#/content/1808`. It is actually a commercial system that is still in beta at the time of writing, but there is a watermarked free *Personal Learning Edition*. Additional info is at `http://www.detoxstudios.com/products/uscript/`.

- Finally, *PlayMaker* is another popular and reasonably priced alternative. It is a bit easier to get started and can be combined with other systems, such as iTween; it is available at: `https://www.assetstore.unity3d.com/#/content/368`

Summary

Scripting is a necessary evil when you need to go beyond the included assets installed with Unity. It might be beneficial to look around the Asset Store to add other tools and scripts to your arsenal, but a decent understanding of scripts is a valuable competence to gain in the long run.

Always strive for short, simple, understandable, and reusable scripts. If you need two unrelated behaviors, they might be better off being split into two scripts. To make scripts reusable for different contexts, give them a rather generic name. `RotateObject` is more versatile than `RotateDoor`. If variables need to be adjusted, provide them as public variables, so they become parameters of the scripts. Reusable scripts never need to be edited during usage, but mainly tweaked by their parameters.

Add easing and *tweening* to improve smoothness and to obtain a visual, modern animation style. If you are pressed in time, you might cut some corners here, but they do provide an overall professional feel to your project, which is really beneficial. If you often need to write scripts that interpolate between values, a system such as *iTween* can be a good alternative, but many cases work well using the `Lerp` methods.

And finally, start with a few basic scripts that you write and know yourself. Do not rush into turnkey systems that take over the whole project. You'd be surprised at how little scripting is really needed for basic, interactive scenes.

Index

Symbols

2D Drafting 9
3D modeling software
about 8-10
workflow 21, 23
3D Warehouse models
loading 70
3PC
about 56-58
and First Person Controller (FPC),
    selecting between 58, 59
setting up 56-58
vs First Person Controller (FPC) 54

A

Adobe Flash 43
advanced textured materials
using 88, 90
Allegorithmic substances 91, 92
animated textures
applying 94
animation clip
creating 42-44
used, for reworking script 106, 107
another level
loading 118, 119
Anti-aliasing effect 49
ArchiCAD
about 17, 18
used, for loading CAD model 29-31
Area light 40
Assets folder 8, 9, 21

Asset Store

about 50
additional tips 119
browsing 50
GUI packages 68
Lightmapping 50
new character, loading 61, 62
URL 50
AutoCAD 9
AutoCAD Architecture 15
Autodesk 3ds Max 9, 19
Autodesk AutoCAD 8
Autodesk Revit 15

B

back-faces
missing 11, 12
basic textured materials
adjusting 83-85
batching
about 78
types 78
batching, types
dynamic batching 78
static batching 78
BIM 8, 14, 15
BIM software
about 14, 15
example 15, 16
real-time solutions 18, 19
using, considerations 17
Blob Shadow 44
Bloom effect 49
Building Information Modeling. *See* **BIM**

C

CAD model
  import settings, controlling 31-33
  loading 29
  loading, ArchiCAD used 29-31
  loading, CINEMA 4D used 29-31
CAD software
  about 8-10
  pitfalls 10
  real-time solutions 18, 19
CAD software, pitfalls
  back-faces, missing 11, 12
  instancing 14
  superfluous geometry 13
  texture coordinates, missing 12, 13
cameras
  switching between 66
  switching between, script used 112
character controller
  3PC 53
  about 53, 54
  First Person Controller (FPC) 53
  setting up 59, 60
Character Motor script 54
CINEMA 4D
  used, for loading CAD model 29-31
COLLADA file format 70
colliders
  using 100-102
Color Correction effect 49
culling 78
custom Skybox
  creating, Skybox tool used 73, 74
custom static model
  using 61
custom third person character
  loading 61
custom trees
  creating, Tree tool used 71-73

D

diffuse shader 33, 83
Digital Content Creation (DCC) 9
Directional light 39

doors
  triggering 96-100
Draw Call Batching
  URL 78
dynamic batching 78

E

elementary glass material
  creating 85-88
elevators
  triggering 96-100
Euler method 99
excessive collision geometry
  avoiding 81

F

faking shadows 44, 45
First Person Controller (FPC)
  about 54, 55
  and 3PC, selecting between 58, 59
  components 54
  scripts 54
  setting up 54, 55
  used, for adding navigation 35
  vs 3PC 53, 54
FPSInput Controller 55
frames per second (FPS) 75
Frustum Culling 76
Fullscreen Image Effects
  about 49
  Anti-aliasing 49
  Color Correction 49
  Lens Flares 49
  Screen Space Ambient Occlusion (SSAO) 49
  Tonemapping 49
  URL 50

G

GameDraw
  URL 19
GameObjects 28, 30
Game tab 27
glass shaders
  reference link 86

Graphical User Interface. *See* GUI
Graphisoft ArchiCAD 15
GUI
  about 107
  displaying, within script 107-109
GUI.Button() method 115
GUI.DrawTexture() method 116
GUI packages, Asset Store 68

H

Hierarchy tab 27

I

iGUI Basic
  about 68
  URL 68
images
  displaying 67
import settings
  controlling 31-33
Inspector tab 27
instancing 14
Integrated Development Environment
      (IDE) 97
intermediate software
  using 10
iTween
  URL 119

K

KMZ file 70

L

landscape
  setting up, Terrain tool used 71
Lens Flares effect 49
Levels of Detail. *See* LOD
LHGS Lighting System 50
light sources
  about 39, 40
  Area light 40
  Directional light 39
  Point light 40
  Spot light 40

Lightmap Manager Lite 50
Lightmapping
  about 46, 48
  basic setup 47
  techniques 49, 50
  URL 46
Lightmapping , Asset Store
  LHGS Lighting System 50
  Lightmap Manager Lite 50
  Lightmapping Extended 50
Lightmapping Extended 50
lights
  toggling 110-112
LightUp
  URL 52
live minimap
  adding 65, 66
  cameras, switching between 66
  turntable camera animation, setting up 67
LOD
  about 77
  URL 77
  using 77

M

material techniques
  about 92
  animated textures, applying 94
  texture mapping, adjusting 93, 94
materials
  about 33, 34
  advanced textured materials 88, 90
  basic textured materials 83-85
  combining 80
  objects, grouping 76
  procedural materials 91
  switching between, script used 115, 116
Maxon CINEMA 4D 9, 19
Mesh Collider 81
meshes
  about 33, 34
  combining 78-80
Mesh Filter 33
Mesh Renderer 33
Mixamo animations
  using 63-65

Mixamo characters
  using 63-65
models. *See also* scenes, optimizing
  updating 19, 20
MonoDevelop 97
Mouse Look script 54
moving platform
  defining 103, 104

N

navigation
  adding, first person controller used 35
Nemetschek VectorWorks 8
new character
  loading 61, 62
NGUI
  about 68
  URL 68

O

objects
  grouping, by materials 76
OnCollisionEnter() event 100
OnGUI() event 107
OnGUI() method 109, 113, 115
OnTriggerEnter() method 109
OnTriggerExit() method 106
opening animation
  refining 102, 103

P

parenting
  problem, solving with 105, 106
Personal Learning Edition
  URL 119
Play button 27
player
  resetting 116, 118
PlayMaker
  URL 119
Point light 40
Point-of-View (POV) camera 112
Prefabs instances
  about 77

characteristics 77
  using 77
pre-rendered models
  about 50, 52
  limitations 51
problem
  solving, with parenting 105, 106
ProBuilder
  URL 19
procedural materials
  Allegorithmic substances 91, 92
  using 91
Project tab 27

R

real-time shadows 40-42
Revit models 21

S

scenes, optimizing
  about 75
  batching 78
  Culling 78
  excessive collision geometry, avoiding 81
  LOD, using 77
  materials, combining 80
  meshes, combining 78-80
  objects, grouping 76
  Prefabs instances, using 77
Scene tab 27
Screen Space Ambient Occlusion (SSAO)
    effect 49
script
  about 95, 96
  GUI, displaying within 107-109
  reworking, animation clip used 106, 107
  used, for switching between cameras 112
  used, materials switching between 115, 116
shaders 33, 34, 83
shadows
  about 40
  faking shadows 44, 45
  real-time shadows 40-42
Skybox tool
  about 73, 74
  used, for creating custom Skybox 73, 74

Spot light 40
Start() method 98, 104
static batching 78
sun light
  adding 34, 35
superfluous geometry 13
switchParent script 105

T

terms of service (ToS) 70
terrain 71
Terrain tool
  about 71
  features 71
  URL, for documentation 71
  used, for setting up landscape 71
text
  displaying 67
texture coordinates
  about 12
  missing 12, 13
texture mapping
  adjusting 93, 94
Third Person Controller. *See* 3PC
Tonemapping effect 49
TPC. *See* 3PC
Tree Creator package 72
Tree tool
  about 71-73
  URL 71
  used, for creating custom trees 71-73
triggers
  using 100-102

Trimble SketchUp 8
turntable camera animation
  setting up 67

U

Unity
  about 8
  Frustum Culling 76
  models, updating 19, 20
  script 95, 96
  Skybox tool 73, 74
  Terrain tool 71
  Tree tool 71-73
  URL, for documentation 8
  workflow 8
Unity project
  CAD model, loading 29
  navigation, adding 35
  recommendations and tips 36
  set up 26, 27, 28
  sun light, adding 34, 35
  tabs 27
Unity project, tab 27
Update() method 98, 100, 102, 104, 113, 114
uScript
  URL 119
UV-texture coordinates 10

V

version control systems (VCS) 8
Visual Editor for iTween
  URL 119

Thank you for buying
Unity for Architectural Visualization

About Packt Publishing

Packt, pronounced 'packed', published its first book *"Mastering phpMyAdmin for Effective MySQL Management"* in April 2004 and subsequently continued to specialize in publishing highly focused books on specific technologies and solutions.

Our books and publications share the experiences of your fellow IT professionals in adapting and customizing today's systems, applications, and frameworks. Our solution based books give you the knowledge and power to customize the software and technologies you're using to get the job done. Packt books are more specific and less general than the IT books you have seen in the past. Our unique business model allows us to bring you more focused information, giving you more of what you need to know, and less of what you don't.

Packt is a modern, yet unique publishing company, which focuses on producing quality, cutting-edge books for communities of developers, administrators, and newbies alike. For more information, please visit our website: www.packtpub.com.

Writing for Packt

We welcome all inquiries from people who are interested in authoring. Book proposals should be sent to author@packtpub.com. If your book idea is still at an early stage and you would like to discuss it first before writing a formal book proposal, contact us; one of our commissioning editors will get in touch with you.

We're not just looking for published authors; if you have strong technical skills but no writing experience, our experienced editors can help you develop a writing career, or simply get some additional reward for your expertise.

SketchUp 7.1 for Architectural Visualization: Beginner's Guide

ISBN: 978-1-84719-946-1   Paperback: 408 pages

Create stunning photo-realistic and artistic visuals of your SketchUp models

1. Create picture-perfect photo-realistic 3D architectural renders for your SketchUp models

2. Post-process SketchUp output to create digital watercolor and pencil art

3. Follow a professional visualization studio workflow

Unity 3.x Scripting

ISBN: 978-1-84969-230-4   Paperback: 292 pages

Write efficient, reusable scripts to build custom characters, game environments, and control enemy AI in your Unity game

1. Make your characters interact with buttons and program triggered action sequences

2. Create custom characters and code dynamic objects and players' interaction with them

3. Synchronize movement of character and environmental objects

Please check **www.PacktPub.com** for information on our titles

Unity Game Development Essentials

ISBN: 978-1-84719-818-1 Paperback: 316 pages

Build fully functional, professional 3D games with realistic environments, sound, dynamic effects, and more!

1. Kick start game development, and build ready-to-play 3D games with ease

2. Understand key concepts in game design including scripting, physics, instantiation, particle effects, and more

3. Test & optimize your game to perfection with essential tips-and-tricks

Unity iOS Game Development Beginners Guide

ISBN: 978-1-84969-040-9 Paperback: 314 pages

Develop iOS games from concept to cash flow using Unity

1. Dive straight into game development with no previous Unity or iOS experience

2. Work through the entire lifecycle of developing games for iOS

3. Add multiplayer, input controls, debugging, in app and micro payments to your game

Please check **www.PacktPub.com** for information on our titles

www.ingramcontent.com/pod-product-compliance
Lightning Source LLC
Chambersburg PA
CBHW060149060326
40690CB00018B/4036